RANDOM
HOUSE

LARGE PRINT

ALSO BY ALAN ALDA

Never Have Your Dog Stuffed

Things I Overheard While Talking to Myself

Things I Overheard While Talking to Myself

ALAN ALDA

RANDOM HOUSE LARGE PRINT

Things I Overheard While Talking to Myself is a work of nonfiction. Some names and identifying details have been changed.

Copyright © 2007 by Mayflower Productions, Inc.

Library of Congress Cataloging-in-Publication Data
Alda, Alan, 1936–
Things I overheard while talking to myself / by Alan Alda.—1st large print ed.
p.   cm.
ISBN 978-0-7393-2757-9 (lg. print)
1. Alda, Alan, 1936–   2. Actors—United States—Biography.   3. Large type books.   I. Title.
PN2287.A45A3 2007
792.02′8092—dc22
[B]
2007029192

Grateful acknowledgment is made to the **Chicago Tribune** for permission to reprint an excerpt from "Advice, Like Youth, Probably Just Wasted on the Young" by Mary Schmich (June 1, 1997), copyright © 1997 by Chicago Tribune.
Reprinted by permission of the **Chicago Tribune**.

www.randomhouse.com/largeprint

FIRST LARGE PRINT EDITION

10 9 8 7 6 5 4 3 2 1

This Large Print edition published in accord with the standards of the N.A.V.H.

Jacket design: Karen Lau
Jacket photographs: courtesy of the author
Frontispiece photograph courtesy of the author

Contents

CONTENTS

Things I Overheard While Talking to Myself

Chapter 1

Things I Overheard While Talking to Myself

I was so glad not to have died that day that I made it my new birthday.

A few hours earlier, I was on top of a mountain outside a small town in Chile when I doubled up in pain from an intestinal obstruction. This is a pain more intense than childbirth, as I was told later by a woman who had enjoyed both. While they carted me down the mountain, the pain was impressive enough to make me feel perfectly okay with dying. I would have been **happy** to die; but as it turned out, this wouldn't be necessary. In a cramped, dingy emergency

3

room, I was examined by a doctor who, by chance, was an expert in exactly my problem. I was lucky, because about a yard of my intestine was dead, and within a couple of hours I would be, too. He opened me up in an emergency surgery that saved my life. I woke up from the operation euphoric. I hugged the doctor and embraced his wife and children, grateful to his whole family for the extra chance at life he had given me. I told everyone that Chile was my new homeland, and I celebrated my new life every chance I got.

But as time passed, a persistent thought kept piercing my euphoria: **What should this new life be like?** This was time I was getting for free, and it seemed to call for freshness.

Not that I was unhappy. During the year I turned sixty-nine, there could hardly have been more good news coming my way. In January, I was nominated for an Oscar; in April, for a Tony; in September, for an Emmy; and in October, the first book I'd written made the bestseller lists. All this in one year. Even my seventieth birthday came and went without a feeling of dread. I was still a kid. I still enjoyed working hard, and my appetites still called to me with the urgency of a kid's. **We must have that dish of pasta,** the food appetite would say. **But this is the third dish of pasta in the same meal,** I'd tell it, secretly delighted by its roguish concupiscence. **Yes, a third dish,** the appetite would say, **and we must** have **it. Now.** Contented as I was, I still wanted to squeeze more juice out of my new life. This was the playful search of a happy appetite, and I realized how lucky I was to be craving more.

I've known people who didn't even know they wanted more, because they felt they simply had nothing. Every once in a while, I think of a moment long ago in a coffee shop in Times Square when the person sitting across from me mentioned he was thinking of killing himself.

He said it casually as he put down his coffee cup. He was a young black man, only recently out of college. I was twenty-five, and he was about twenty-two. We had met a few days earlier at a gathering of idealistic young people hoping to end nuclear testing. We had been talking about how completely dim the prospects were of our group having any success in slowing the arms race. Then our conversation turned somehow from the destruction of cities in a nuclear firestorm to the subject of his own life. That's when he put down his cup and said, with the air of someone announcing he was considering going off cream for skim milk, "I've been thinking that I might kill myself."

I was stunned. "You can't do that."

He looked surprised. "Why not?"

"You don't have the right to kill yourself."

"Of course I do. It's my life. I can do what I want with it."

"No, you can't. You can't do that to the people around you. You can't leave them with grief and a dead body. You don't have the right to do that to anyone."

He thought about that for a moment. "Yes, I do. It's my body."

"Look. You're smart, you're educated. You have a life ahead of you. A career." I didn't even know what he did for a living, but he was smart. He'd be able to get along in anything he chose to do.

"Well, I might go for that," he said, "but I might kill myself. I haven't decided. It's just an option."

When someone's heading down that dark tunnel, how do you call him back? Certainly my indignation wasn't having any effect. I lost track of him not long after that and didn't find out if he ever acted on his thoughts, but I always wished I could have said something to turn him away from that darkness.

A decade later, I was surprised to be facing that same frustration. I was acting on television in M*A*S*H, and after a shaky start, the show was an enormous hit. Mail started coming in by the bagful. One afternoon, I sat in a canvas chair on the set between shots and sorted through a handful of letters. There was a note in a pink envelope, addressed to me in tiny, cramped handwriting. I opened it and started reading:

**Please help me. I don't know what to do.
I feel like killing myself.**

The writer was a girl, probably a teenager. Her handwriting was neat and controlled, but her thoughts were all over the place. I was the one person, she said, who could help. Would I please write back as soon as possible with some words that would keep her from ending her life?

A few weeks later, a letter came in from a young man thinking of suicide. Then another, from someone else. There were about a dozen during the run of the show, and I answered them as well as I could. One man wrote back, saying my letter had helped him to reconsider and now he was glad to be alive—but I wondered about the ones I didn't hear from. They had seemed to be looking for some kind of meaning in their lives. Had they found it?

Once the show became successful, invitations started coming in asking me to pronounce a few words to live by at college commencements and even offering honorary degrees. I instinctively recoiled. It was flattering, but flattery is the doorway to embarrassment. What did I have to say to people that was worth the time it took to listen to it? The more successful our show got, the more they asked me to come and talk. It was all out of proportion. So I went and talked. I couldn't resist the flattery. But I worked on those speeches with more diligence than I'd ever used on anything before.

As my children were growing up, and later with my grandchildren, I would look for those pleasurable moments when I could call up something that would feel like passing on a little wisdom. In all of these talks, public and private, of course, I probably hadn't really been talking to other people. I'm sure I was really talking to **myself.**

Couched in jokes and colloquial banter, my advice was always there: the pill in the pudding.

But it wasn't such a bad pill. I was often trying to see how young people could guard themselves from a feeling later on that their lives had been a pointless passing of time. The same thing, in a way, that I was now trying to guard against myself.

I started rummaging in the back of my mind and in the bottoms of drawers for old speeches and other things I'd said that meant something to me. And I wanted to figure out the context. What was going on in our lives then that led me to say what I said? I felt a little tingle of excitement in my belly. This would be fun.

For some reason, just before I take a look inside myself I always think it's going to be fun. This is a particular form of narcissistic madness, actors' division. Before I knew it, I was tangled up in an unexpected and thorny question. It came at me in plain words one night, in that sullen calm before sleep. This is the calm that has two doors: One leads to dreams and the other to thoughts, and the door to thoughts is the one that goes nowhere.

With teeth scrubbed, the bathroom light switched off, and just before the light in your brain flickers out, there is a special depth to the dark. It was in that thick quiet that I heard a question move forward from the back of my head.

So tell me, the voice asked, **are you living a life of meaning?**

Oh, please, I thought.

No, really, said the voice. **If it should happen that you don't wake up tomorrow, will this have been a life that meant something?**

I really hadn't expected this. I was just looking for a little more juice. **Meaning?** Was this voice kidding me? Hadn't this year been the essence of a meaningful life? I was successful in my work. My children and grandchildren were thriving, and my wife and I had never been happier. Arlene and I were taking time to do idle, playful things on the spur of the moment. We took an afternoon off to go look at Grand Central Station, just because we hadn't seen it in thirty years. And then we spent an hour in the Museum of Modern Art, which we hadn't seen since they fixed it up. Then we walked for blocks, looking for a taxi, and when we got to Central Park and still couldn't get a cab, we smelled horses behind us. We turned and saw the hansom cabs lined up on Fifty-ninth Street and decided to go home by horse and carriage. We grinned for the whole trip.

It was a perfect life. So why would I wonder what the **meaning** of it was? But the damn question wouldn't go away. Once it got hold of me, it didn't just linger—it pulled at my lapels, jabbed its finger in my chest. Demanded an answer.

But meaning is a tricky thing. I sat next to a young woman on a plane once who bombarded me for five hours with how she had decided to be born again and so should I. I told her I was glad for her, but I hadn't used up being born the first time. Nothing stopped her. She was married to an acquaintance of mine, and I couldn't turn her off. I left the plane with an ache in my head the size of a grapefruit. I'm certain she led a life that was meaningful to her and had just had five meaningful hours of it. But that didn't mean she was living the good life. And for five hours neither was I. Fight for what you believe in, they say. Serve a higher purpose than yourself. This will give you fulfillment. It can also turn you into the lady on the plane. Or even a terrorist. Terrorists may feel more purpose in their lives than other people do, but that doesn't mean terrorists are any better off; and neither are the rest of us.

If I was going looking for meaning, I didn't want meaning that would betray other people, and I also didn't want it to betray me. I wanted it to last. Billy Rose wrote a song a long time ago that asked:

Does the spearmint lose its flavor on the bedpost overnight?
If you chew it in the morning, will it be too hard to bite?

That was me. I didn't want to wake up someday and find that what had once given meaning to my life was as stale and tasteless as yesterday's gob of gum.

For a while in my teens, I was sure I had it. It was about getting to heaven. If heaven existed and lasted forever, then a mere lifetime spent scrupulously following orders was a small investment for an infinite payoff. One day, though, I realized I was no longer a believer, and realizing that, I couldn't go back. Not that I lost the urge to pray. Occasionally, even after I stopped believing, I might send off a quick memo to the Master of the Universe, usually on a matter needing urgent attention, like **Oh, God, don't let us crash.** These were automatic expulsions of words, brief SOS messages from the base of my brain. They were similar to the short prayers that were admired by the church in my Catholic boyhood, which they called "ejaculations." I always liked the idea that you could shorten your time in purgatory with each ejaculation; what boy wouldn't find that a comforting idea? But my effort to keep the plane in the air by talking to God didn't mean I suddenly was overcome with belief, only that I was scared. Whether I'd wake up in heaven someday or not, whatever meaning I found would have to occur first on this end of eternity.

When I was young, I noticed that the Greeks had asked what the "Good Life" was, and their question stuck in my mind. As I read more, I came across vastly different answers. There was Thomas Aquinas, who seemed to think a good life would be rewarded later; there was the ancient rabbi who said the reward of a good life is a good life; and there was Ernest Hemingway, who said if it feels good, it's good. There was a cacophony of opinion about what the good life was and what it was good for. Still, the question remained: **We live. We die. What's in between?** I had a feeling the answer would come to me if I listened in on the things I'd been telling myself. Not just in formal talks in front of crowds, but also in those chance moments on a walk, or driving in a car with a child, when the right words fell together and I said something I didn't know I knew.

I picked up a pile of yellowed typewritten papers, moved over to an easy chair, and started reading.

And as I turned the pages, the gates opened and the memories flooded in.

Chapter 2

Lingering at the Door

I fell deeply in love with her. When we brought her home from the hospital, I carried her up the narrow stairs to our second-floor apartment as Arlene walked ahead of me, climbing slowly against the pull of her stitches. We were in Ohio, where I was making sixty dollars a week at the Cleveland Playhouse. With local commercials, I could sometimes bring it up to eighty a week, and we had four sunny rooms and a couch we'd bought for five dollars at the Salvation Army that was comfortable, if lumpy, and equipped with a set of fleas.

Very soon, our freshly born girl looked us in the eye and smiled toothlessly. They said in those days that babies didn't smile, that it was just gas. But we knew that in spite of science and all of nature, she was smiling at us. It wasn't gas; it was love beyond the limits of anatomy.

We called her Eve. For us, she was the first woman ever born.

During the day, while I was at rehearsal, Arlene would walk down the empty streets of our neighborhood with Eve in her carriage, partly to get some air but mainly in the hope that someone would pass by and stop to look at our amazing baby. At night, when I wasn't onstage, I would read Sholom Aleichem stories aloud to Arlene while she cooked dinner and Eve slept in her crib.

As the soup simmered, Tevye delivered his milk and our girl slept quietly until she woke and called for her late-night meal. There was no doubt in that moment what our purpose in life was. Arlene would make her own milk delivery, and then I would walk barefoot on the midnight linoleum, our daughter slung over my shoulder, urging up a burp. There was no question that she, with her gummy smile, was all the reason we needed to be alive.

When she was six months old, we moved back to New York, where I took part-time jobs while trying to find work on Broadway. After three months as a doorman outside a ritzy restaurant near Rockefeller Center, I auditioned for a part that consisted of five lines of dialogue. I got the job and was completely thrilled. It was my first Broadway show. I gave back my elaborate doorman's costume and began a month of rehearsals, during which time I must have said my five lines five hundred ways. Herman Shumlin was directing the show, a thin comedy called **Only in America.** Shumlin was a tall man in his sixties, as thin as the play, but with a sense of humor he had apparently picked up watching Gestapo officers in war movies of the forties. Every time I read one of my lines, he turned his bald head in my direction and looked as if he were going to ask me for my papers. He never smiled. Instead, he would hold his forehead and wince. After a few days, I realized he was constantly in the middle of a migraine attack, and I could see that the whole process of rehearsal was torture for him. It wasn't all that great for anyone else, either.

In those days, plays went out of town to get the kinks out of a show. Ours was composed almost entirely of kinks, so they had to pick and choose which ones to drop. I was hoping they weren't going to drop the five that made up my whole part. Arlene and I packed up Eve and her carriage and got on the train for Philadelphia, where we rented the cheapest room we could find. It seemed to me that the show wouldn't run more than a week or two when we got back to New York, so we wanted to save as much cash as we could while we were on the road. We found a charming hovel that was almost a replica of the rooms I had stayed in as a child, traveling with my mother and father on the burlesque circuit. The walls were covered with wooden slats painted a shade of green that must have been a high point in the history of bile.

After a couple of days in this cheerful place, Arlene caught the flu. She was unable to get out of bed and needed to sleep from morning until night. We were rehearsing onstage for the first time on the full set, and I had to be there, so I put Eve in her carriage and took her to the theater. I kept her backstage, out of the sight of Shumlin, who I felt pretty sure would see her and start clutching at his head. But then I heard my cue coming up, and I had to run onstage. I asked the other actors to watch Eve for me. They were thrilled. Actors love babies. They're a perfect audience. As I looked over my shoulder, I saw Eve in her carriage surrounded by six actors cooing and making faces. She looked a little bewildered.

I was playing a telephone lineman, and my part went like this: I came onstage, said a line intended to make the audience laugh, then climbed up a telephone pole, where I said two or three lines whose main purpose was to call attention to the fact that the producer had paid for a real telephone pole; then I hung there for twenty minutes while the play went on before I climbed down, said another funny line, and left. At this rehearsal, I got up to the top of the pole and spent my time hoping Eve was all right in the middle of the crush of actors. After only a minute or two, though, a loud wail rose from behind the scenery. It spread across the stage and hit the back wall. Then another wail. This one made it all the way to the box office in the lobby. Everyone stood completely still. Shumlin turned his bald head and looked up at me. I tried to look apologetic.

"I imagine that would be your child," he said.

"Uh, yes. I'm sorry."

Then the unbelievable happened. A gentle smile spread over Shumlin's face, possibly the first in his life. "Why don't you go look after her? We'll work on something else."

I shimmied down the pole and ran to Eve. Her lower lip was up, and the corners of her mouth were down. She reached out her arms for me. I hugged her, and in a few minutes she was contented again, but that scene came back to me many times as Eve grew up. The actors had tried to entertain her, because entertaining is what we do. But she hadn't needed entertainment, she'd needed safety. Years later, I wondered if I had given in too many times to that same actor's impulse. I'd certainly entertained my children, probably to the point of being their playmate. Once, when Eve was four, we were standing in the basement having one of those endless arguments.

"You have to clean up this mess you made."

"No, I **don't** have to clean it up."

"Yes, you do."

"No, I don't."

"You do."

"I don't."

Finally, I called upstairs. "Arlene, will you come down here and tell her I'm the boss?" It kind of took the authority out of the exchange.

I had always been moved by Alan Jay Lerner's

lyric from **Camelot**'s "How to Handle a Woman." The way to handle a woman, he said, was to love her, simply love her. Love her. Love her. It took me a while to figure out that that's probably the best way to handle a child, too. But I really liked trying to teach them and stimulate their minds.

From the time they were able to talk, I was always starting dinner conversations with them about world events, but our three girls only stared at me, thinking it was one of my actorish riffs that just wasn't that amusing. If they waited long enough, I'd change the channel. I was flummoxed. I wondered: How did the Kennedys accomplish all the dinner conversations we always read about? How did they get **their** children to talk?

When Eve was ready to graduate from college, I was asked to speak at her commencement, and I said, yes, of course I'll talk. I was more than touched. I would finally be able to talk about anything I wanted and she'd have to listen.

But what would I talk about? As the day came closer, I sat and wrote on the porch of our room on a Caribbean island, where I was directing my first movie. I had all the worries of a first-time director, plus a rainy season that had put us behind schedule. But in every spare moment, I sat on the porch and tried to figure out what I'd say. There was plenty going on in the world, if I'd wanted to start another of my dinner conversations. The past ten years had been hard to take. It was 1980, and there was already a frightening amount of terrorism in the world. I recently looked it up on the Internet. In those ten years, there had been over six thousand terrorist events, bombings mostly, that had killed 3,500 people and wounded 7,600. This was supposed to make the world a better place. The Equal Rights Amendment was about to run out its time limit. Eve knew I had worked hard for ten years trying to help get it ratified and that I had traveled to state after state, lobbying state legislators. Eve knew how much it had meant to Arlene and me, and now, three states short of ratification, it was becoming clear it would not become part of the Constitution.

I had plenty to talk about, but what I most wanted to say to her were things that were hard to put into words. They were things I'd wanted to say all along, but somehow they didn't come out early on.

Eve graduated from college on a hot day in May. I walked out onto the sun-washed green, dotted with white folding chairs and people fanning themselves in the late spring heat. I knew I wouldn't be able to tell Eve what I wanted her to hear by talking to her as part of her whole class. She'd get lost in the crowd. So, instead, I spoke directly to her. I called her by name and poured out my heart and hoped that the other graduates would see that, through her, I was talking to them, too.

Deep in our hearts we know that the best things said come last. People will talk for hours, saying nothing much, and then linger at the door with words that come with a rush from the heart. We're all gathered at a doorway today. It's the end of something and the beginning of something else.

We linger with our hand on the knob, searching for words, but the best things said slip out unheralded and often preceded by the words Oh, by the way. **Patients can talk to their therapists for an hour, hardly saying anything, but just as they're leaving, they'll turn at the door and say, "Oh, by the way," and in one sentence reveal everything they've been avoiding for fifty minutes. Doorways are where the truth is told.**

As we stand in one today, these are my parting words to my daughter Eve. They'll come in a rush, because there are so many things I want to tell you, Eve. And the first one is: Don't be scared. My guess is you're feeling a little uncertain today. That's okay; I'm uncertain, too. You're an adult when the leaders of the world are behaving like children. The tune of the day is the song of the terrorist: humane concerns inhumanely expressed.

And you're facing this sooner than I thought you would. Suddenly, you're a grown woman. The day before yesterday, you were a baby I was afraid to hold because you seemed so fragile. Yesterday, you broke your small eight-year-old arm. Only this morning, you were a teenager.

As we get older, the only thing that speeds up is time. But as much as time is a thief, it also leaves something in exchange. With time comes experience—and however uncertain you may be about the rest of the world, you have the chance to keep getting better at the things you work at.

And that's something else I want to tell you as we stand in this doorway today. Love your work. If you always put your heart into everything you do, you can't lose. Whether or not you wind up making a lot of money, you will have had a wonderful time, and no one will ever be able to take that away from you.

I want to squeeze things great and small into this lingering good-bye. I want to tell you to keep laughing. I used to be afraid that writing and acting in comedies might be a frivolous occupation, but when I think of all the good that laughing does people, I get the feeling that making people laugh can be noble work. You have a wonderful laugh. You gurgle when you laugh. Keep gurgling. There are people who think that the only thing that separates humans from the rest of the animals is their ability to laugh. I'm not so sure anything separates us from the rest of the animals except our extreme egotism that leads us to think that they're the animals and we're not. But I notice that when people are laughing, they're generally not killing one another. So keep laughing, and if you can, get other people to join you in laughter.

I have this helpless urge to pass on maxims to you. But we live in new times. Strange times. Even the Golden Rule doesn't seem adequate to pass on to a daughter. There should be something added to it. You know how I love amendments. You knew I wanted to amend the Constitution, but you probably didn't know I wanted to amend the Golden Rule as well. Here's my Golden Rule for a tarnished age: Be fair with others; then keep after them until they're fair with you.

It's a complex world. I hope you'll learn to make distinctions. You know how much I love logic. I always felt that the most important parts of my education were learning to reason and to use language. That's why when you were a very little girl I started trying to give you lessons in logic. I smile when I think that to this day, you can still remember what I taught you as a child—the first rule of logic: A thing cannot both be and not be at the same time and in the same respect. (In your head, you're saying that along with me right now, aren't you?) I hope you'll always make distinctions. A peach is not its fuzz, a toad is not its warts, a person is not his or her crankiness. If we can make distinctions, we can be tolerant, and we can get to the heart of our problems instead of wrestling endlessly with their gross exteriors. And once you make a habit of making distinctions, you'll begin challenging your own assumptions. Your assumptions are your windows on the world. Scrub them off every once in a while or the light won't come in. If you challenge your own, you won't be so quick to accept the unchallenged assumptions of others. You'll be a lot less likely to be caught up in bias or prejudice or be influenced by people who ask you to hand over your brains, your soul, or your money because they have everything all figured out for you.

I want you to be as smart as you can, but remember: It's always better to be wise than to be smart. And don't be upset that it takes a long, long time to find wisdom, because nobody knows where wisdom can be found. It tends to break out at unexpected times, like a rare virus to which mostly people with compassion and understanding are susceptible.

The door is inching a little closer toward the latch, and I still haven't said it. You'll be gone, and I won't have found the words. Let me dig a little deeper.

Let me go back to when I was in college. There were ideas that had power for me then—maybe they will for you now. I'd almost forgotten how much one of those ideas meant to me—how much I wrote about it and thought about it. It was the essence of a philosophy that was very popular at the time, and it's one of the most helpful and cheerful ideas I've ever heard.

It's this: Life is absurd and meaningless and full of nothingness. Possibly this doesn't strike you as helpful and cheerful, but I think it is—because it's honest and because it goads you on.

I had a teacher in those days who saw me with a book by Jean-Paul Sartre under my arm, and he said, "Be careful. If you read too much of that, you'll start walking around dressed in black, looking wan, doing nothing for the rest of your life." Well, I did read the book, and as it turned out, I'm tanned and lovely, I'm rich and productive, and I'm happy like nobody's business.

Maybe it was my natural optimism at work, but what I saw and warmed to in the existentialist's writings was that life is meaningless unless you bring meaning to it; it's up to us to create our own existence. Unless you do something, unless you make something, it's as though you aren't there. Existentialism was supposed to be the philosophy of despair. But not to me. To me, it was the essence of hope—because it touched the cold, hard stone at rock bottom and saw it as a way to push off it and bounce back up again.

Back when I was reading the existentialists, we heard the news that God was dead, but now Sartre is dead, too, and so is Camus—and, in a way, so is the optimism at the heart of their pessimism. The distressing reality is that twenty-five years ago when I was in college, we all talked about nothingness but moved into a world of effort and endeavor. And now no one much talks about nothingness, but the world itself, the one you will move into, is filled with it. If you want, there's plenty you can do to turn that nothing into something. You can dig into the world and push it into better shape.

For one thing, you can clean the air and water. Some people have said that lead poisoning was a major cause of the fall of the Roman Empire, because the ruling class had their food cooked in expensive pots that were lined with lead. They didn't know any better, but we don't have that excuse. Now, almost two thousand years later, we've hit upon the incredibly clever idea of getting rid of our industrial waste by putting it into our food. Not directly, of course; that would be too expensive. First they put it in the ground—then it goes into the water, and the next thing you know, you're eating a sludgeburger. If you want, you can do something about that.

Or you can try to make the justice system work. You can bring the day a little closer when the rich and privileged have to live by the same standards as the poor and the outcast.

Or you can try to keep the tiger of war away from our gates for a while longer. You can do what you can to keep old men from sending children away to die. They're tuning up for the song of war again. They're making preparations and trial excursions. They're tickling our anger. They're asking us if we're ready to pour the cream of our youth out onto the ground, where it will seep into the earth and disappear forever. You can tell them we're not. The time to stop the next war is now—before it starts.

If you want to take absurdity by the neck and shake it till its brains rattle, you can try to find out how it is that people can see one another as less than human. How can people be capable of both nurture and torture? How we can worry and fret about a little girl caught in a mine shaft, spending days and nights getting her out, but then burn a village to the ground and destroy all its people without blinking? If you're interested, you can question that, too, and you can try to find out why people all over the world, of every country, of every class, of every religion, have at one time or another found it so easy to use other people like farm animals, to make them suffer, and to just plain do away with them.

And while you're at it, there's something else you can do. You can pass on the torch that's been carried from Seneca Falls. Remember that every right you have as a woman was won for you by women fighting hard. Everything else you have is a privilege, not a right. A privilege is given and taken away at the pleasure of those in power. There are little girls being born right now who may not have the same rights you do when they grow up unless you do something to maintain and extend the range of equality for women. The soup of civilized life is a nourishing stew, but it doesn't keep stocked on its own. Put something back in the pot as you leave for the people in line behind you.

There are, of course, hundreds of things you can work on, and they're all fairly impossible to achieve, so there's plenty to keep you busy for the rest of your life. I can't promise you this will ever completely reduce that sense of absurdity, but it may get it down to a manageable level. It will allow you once in a while to take a glorious vacation from nothingness and bask in the feeling that all in all, things do seem to be moving forward.

I want you to be potent; to do good when you can and to hold your wit and your intelligence like a shield against other people's wantonness. I want you to be strong and aggressive and tough and resilient and full of feeling.

I want you to have chutzpah.

Nothing important was ever accomplished without chutzpah. Columbus had chutzpah. The signers of the Declaration of Independence had chutzpah. Do you wonder if you're strong enough? Sure you are. Get a little perspective. Look up at the stars swirling in the heavens and see how tiny and puny they look. They're gigantic explosions, but from where we are, they're just these insignificant little dots. If you step back from things far enough, you realize how important and powerful you are. Be bold. Let the strength of your desire give force and moment to your every step. They may laugh at you if you don't discover India. Let them laugh. India's already there. You'll come back with a brand-new America. Move with all of yourself. When you embark for strange places, don't leave any of yourself safely on shore. Have the nerve to go into unexplored territory. Be brave enough to live life creatively. The creative is the place where no one else has ever been. It is not the previously known. You have to leave the city of your comfort and go into the wilderness of your intuition. You can't get there by bus, only by hard work and risk and by not quite knowing what you're doing, but what you'll discover will be wonderful. What you'll discover will be yourself.

Those are my parting words as today's door closes softly between us. There will be other partings and other last words in our lives, so if today's lingering at the threshold didn't quite speak the unspeakable, maybe the next one will.

I'll let you go now.

So long, be happy.
Oh, by the way, I love you.

They awarded me a Connecticut College chair that day. An actual chair. I kept it by the front door for years to remind me of the afternoon I'd been able to open my heart to our first child. But as the years went on and I passed the chair in my comings and goings, I noticed that almost every problem I'd mentioned to her that day, almost everything I'd said she could work on fixing, had got worse. As our lives went on, the hopes I had for her grew even higher, but everything I'd mentioned about the world had sunk below sea level.

Eve went on to become a social worker, and she ran for office in her town and won. She did dig into the world; and if she couldn't make it better, it wasn't for lack of trying. But now for her, as it has been for me, there **will** be one sure way of finding purpose in her life. Now she has children.

And now I see, and so does she, that our job is not to shape them and badger them, but to love them.

Simply love them.

Love them.

Love them.

35

Chapter 3

Playing in the Street

We were playing on a trash heap down by the East River. We were four years old, and the three of us had spent the afternoon climbing over rusty shards of iron and steel. After a while, bored with scrambling across the debris, one of the other boys started taunting his brother, as brothers will do, and they began hurling insults at each other. Before long, they were hurling bits of scrap metal. I was between them, watching. One of them picked up a tin can and cocked his arm, threatening to throw it. The lid had been cut with an old-fashioned can opener and bent back. Its burred edge was like a sharp, circular saw.

I held up my hand and said, "Stop!" I wanted him to stop, but I also meant to be funny. I was imitating the comics I had watched from the wings of the burlesque theaters where my father worked as a singer and straight man. In burlesque, people threw things and doused one another with seltzer. The straight men even took the comics by the neck and threw them across the stage, but no one ever got hurt. My "Stop!" was more like a line in a comedy sketch than a real-life command.

It would have been smarter to get out of the way. The jagged top of the tin can came toward me end over end and sliced open an inch-long patch of skin on my head. Within seconds, my scalp was gushing and my body was covered with blood.

The boys quickly sobered and walked me back to the brownstone where we lived and handed me over to my mother. For years I had a scar where the slice intersected the part in my hair. This gave me my first lesson in public speaking: Say what you mean and mean what you say—and don't expect to get a laugh when they're hurling metal at you.

I stepped up to the microphone at Emerson College in Boston on a day in May, hoping to say what I meant and not have to duck. I was forty now, and M*A*S*H had been on the air for five years. Emerson, a communications college, had asked me to speak to the graduating class, who, I was sure, would be sitting there, hoping the commencement speaker wouldn't trash their day. I thought for a long time about what I'd say to them.

It was 1977, and the Vietnam War had ended four years earlier, with some wounds that had not yet hardened into scars. Watergate had forced Nixon out of office, and the shock of it was still with us. We were not that far removed from the years of assassination and unrest. The deaths of Martin Luther King and Bobby Kennedy, and the riots at the Democratic National Convention in 1968, and the protests at Kent State in 1970 in which four students had been shot and killed had stunned us, and we had not fully recovered. Little yellow smiley-face buttons began showing up everywhere not long after Kent State, and soon fifty million of them had been sold. It was as if the country were signaling itself that it had suffered enough.

Our recent history had been tumultuous, yet

I'd be speaking to a generation that was changing. They had turned away from boisterous demonstrations and were beginning to think more about their own careers.

I wanted to say something that wouldn't just bounce off them, something they could take in and connect to. I took off my mortarboard, looked into their faces, and dove in.

I hope I can say something that will have some meaning for you. I hope I can say something that will set you so on fire, you'll never forget it. Because twenty-one years ago when I was on your side of the academic footlights and I was graduating from college, we were addressed by several distinguished people who gave us encouragement and wisdom and wit, and I can't remember a damn thing anybody said.

Well, I'm going to tell you something you'll remember. You may not believe this as you sit here now, but at some point in your lives a lot of you are going to look up from your work and wonder: "What's the point of it all?" You'll wonder how much you're really getting accomplished and how

much it all means. I think it's safe to say that most of you will experience this.

The sentence "What's the purpose of all this?" is written in big letters over the door of the Midlife Crisis Butcher Shop. You can't miss it as you lug the carcass of your worldly success through the door to have it dressed and trimmed and placed in little plastic packages so you can dazzle people with it in your showcase. "What's the purpose of all this?" You may ask yourself that question next year or twenty years from now. But when you do, you'll remember what I'm going to tell you now.

Well, that was a little brash. I don't know why I thought anything I said would be remembered. This is how you remember things:

A few weeks after I got my head split open on the trash heap at the age of four, I let myself be inspired by the comics again and got another lesson I wasn't expecting. I was outside our brownstone apartment on Thirty-second Street, sitting on the running board of a car, chatting with a girl my age. I liked her, and I decided to make her laugh. Who knows what I said. There were all kinds of rude words and rough humor that passed between the comics and strippers out on the road. I didn't know what most of it meant, but I knew it made people laugh, and I tried some of it out on the running-board girl. She pulled back her hand and whacked me across the face. My cheek stung, and my eyes teared instantly. She looked over at her mother, who was sitting across the sidewalk on the stoop, watching us. Her mother said, "Hit him again." She hit me again. What had I said? I never found out.

But the sting of the slap remained on my face as a reminder that I was an outsider; our language wasn't spoken here. Jim McGaugh, the memory researcher, told me that centuries ago, when a village wanted the memory of an important event to pass down to the next generation, the villagers would take a seven-year-old who had witnessed the event and throw him in the river. They would rescue him before he drowned, but the shock of the experience registered the day in his memory for the rest of his life. The little girl's slap did the same for me. For a long time, I remembered that I was not one of these people. I never abandoned the comic end of the running board, but the slap was one of the signals I got from the civilian world that I'd have to learn to modify my sense of humor to fit the company I was in.

So there was no chance the graduates would remember what I said that day, unless I took them over to the Charles River and threw them in. But I did get their attention. Now there was the little thing of what I was going to tell them. It was going to be something personal. I had gone for the personal the first time I spoke in public, and I never veered from it, even though the results that first time were nearly as memorable as the slap in the face had been.

I was dry at the back of my throat that day. I wanted to make a good impression, but I didn't stand much of a chance. I was in a citywide speech competition, and the topic was "Tolerance: How Can We Promote It in Burbank?" Not that tough in itself, but I was fourteen and up against my school's football hero, who was three years older than me. He was a tall, good-looking quarterback with a smooth style. He had the authority of someone who called the plays and knew his calls would be followed. Pretty much all I had was sincerity, which kind of paled against Strong and Handsome.

We were giving our talks in a large room above a catering hall, with the mayor and his staff judging us. The afternoon sun spilled across the bare wooden floor, and the judges looked at us from the other end of the room with polite neutrality. Tony, the football hero, was up first. He made his way effortlessly, and I thought glibly, down a list of public service announcements and essay contests that could inspire support for tolerance in the town of Burbank. I could see the judges nodding. The quarterback sat down, confident that he had scored.

I rose and called a smile up to my face. They smiled back, politely. I wasn't going to try to use humor, but the only other tool I had was a kind of passionate naïveté. I looked at the mayor and his aides, and I said, "The people who can do something about tolerance in this town are right here in this room." I could see their smiles tighten just a little. This was probably not what they were expecting.

Then I got personal. "When you walk down the street and someone approaches in the other direction, do you play a game, wondering what their ethnic background is, or their religion? Does that matter? Couldn't we, each one of us, see people for who they are? Wouldn't that be the real beginning of tolerance in Burbank?"

I was suggesting that, generally, people should look inward, but as I talked, I was getting a vague feeling of doom. The mayor and his aides were beginning to look uncomfortable, as if I were questioning their own sense of tolerance. I saw the danger, but pluck rose in me like fetid flood-waters and I couldn't stop. When it was over, they awarded me second prize, which wasn't all that bad, even though there were only two of us in the contest.

I decided to leave public speaking for a while. Instead, I joined the school chorus because I had a crush on the nun who conducted the singing group and also because it got me out of study hall, where they actually expected you to study. Spending an hour watching Sister Mary Alice waving her arms at us seemed much more pro-ductive. The only thing I didn't like was that she had seated me next to Tony, the football hero. And he was even more self-assured about singing than he was about public speaking. As we prac-ticed, I was surprised to find out that harmoniz-ing required you to sing a completely different tune from what other people were singing. You had your part and they had theirs, and there were little marks on a musical staff in the songbook that you were supposed to be able to read. I had thought singing was just something you did, but this seemed a lot like study hall. My father sang for the half-naked chorus girls in burlesque without agonizing over it. Why couldn't **I**?

I opened my mouth and sang what sounded to me close enough to what the people in my section were singing. But I kept drifting halfway between what they were doing and the melody. I was singing, as they say, in the cracks.

The football player listened to me struggling and deftly put me away. He never said I stank; he just launched into a conspiratorial account of how some people in the chorus had no idea how to read music. "This is what they think a half-tone interval is," he said, and sang a couple of notes. "And this is a whole tone to them." He sang another two notes, which sounded to me exactly like the first two. I nodded my head, only vaguely aware I was being mocked.

A couple of weeks later, the ax fell. Sister Mary Alice made us sing a passage over and over. "Somebody's flat," she said. "Who is it?"

There were no volunteers, so she asked only the left side of the room to sing, then the right side. Then the top half of the right side, then the bottom half. She was zeroing in. I knew it must be me, but I couldn't stand the thought that I was letting her down. I had a crush on her. I dreamed about her. I couldn't be the one who sang flat.

But I was. She asked me into her office, where she explained gently that different people have different skills, while I ignored the tears in the back of my throat. As I left the chorus for good, the football player winked at me. He managed to get more derision into that one little wink than I thought was possible.

My revenge was going back to class and getting into politics. I was beginning to be noticed in school because I could get even more laughs than the official class clown. He was Tom, an admirable boy who knew how to look surprised while he fell over backward in a chair and tumbled out of it. He taught me how to fall backward in a straight-backed chair, and I felt we were part of the brotherhood of pratfall artists. We amused the class so much, they elected us both president of our respective homerooms.

The election taught me one of the great uses for politics: You could transform the slights dished out by one or two people in your life into the comforting praise of a large number of others who, in voting for you, were saying they liked you. At fourteen, I didn't know much more than that about the real world of politics. On the other hand, there may not **be** much more than that.

By the time I got to college and was about the same age as the kids I'd be speaking to at Emerson, I had only a hazy understanding of what was going on in Washington. I'd heard of Senator Joe McCarthy, who was in full flower during my college days at Fordham, and I wasn't immune to the seductive perfume of his tirades. I remember walking with a friend along a campus path. He talked with real feeling about how Mc-Carthy was attacking the country's fundamental values. I didn't read the newspapers much in those days, but I knew from headlines in the **Daily News** that McCarthy was accusing a lot of people of being Communists. McCarthy had a certain appeal for me. This was a time in my life when I was looking for refuge from a childhood of uncertainty. Since I was a baby, I hadn't been able to count on my mother, who was schizo-phrenic, paranoid, and alcoholic. She loved me, certainly, but her version of reality shifted from hour to hour. I was looking for a rational uni-verse, and one that included layers of authority that would be consistent from top to bottom. The church had it all figured out with a formula that was tightly reasoned, once you accepted its first premises on faith. So when my friend agonized over Joe McCarthy, it didn't seem like a difficult question.

As we strolled down the path in the late afternoon sun, I said I didn't think McCarthy was so bad. It seemed to me that a country had the right to defend itself against its enemies. My friend was silent for a while, but I could see his crestfallen face. Finally, he spoke softly. "These people aren't its enemies. They're its citizens."

The quiet pain in my friend's voice registered with me. It was one of a number of small moments that made me wonder how useful prepackaged answers were. I started asking questions; and that led, as it often does, to questioning the people in charge.

I was becoming convinced that the world wasn't running the way it ought to and that I probably ought to fix it. When you're an only child, brought up in the spotlight of show business, you think like that.

There certainly was plenty about our world that needed fixing. A few years after I'd graduated from college and had finally found work on Broadway, we were in the ice age of the cold war. The Soviet Union and the United States already had enough weapons aimed at each other to blow up several planets, yet they kept testing bigger and better ones. I helped form a tiny but industrious committee of theater people who hoped, just a little quixotically, to be helpful in bringing an end to nuclear testing. We would do this by collecting signatures from other Broadway actors on a petition. We were going to mail the petition to the leaders of both the United States and the Soviet Union, who had the hotlines open—waiting to hear what Broadway actors had to say about nuclear arms. It was a gesture that was both entirely humanitarian and completely pointless, but at the time it felt satisfying.

I was acting in **Purlie Victorious,** a farcical, passionate romp written by Ossie Davis and starring Ossie and Ruby Dee. Ossie's play put racial stereotypes onstage in order to lacerate them with gusto. I was playing Charley Cotchipee, the idealistic son of the plantation owner. I was twenty-five that year and just as callow as Charley. I went with my petition in hand and knocked on Ruby's dressing room door, certain that she would sign and march with us the next week. I told her how we were going to get hundreds, maybe thousands, of signatures from theater artists and send them to the nuclear powers and stop the testing of nuclear weapons, which was a peril to humanity. My pitch was high-flown and feverish. As she listened, I saw a weariness come over her face. I was confused. Surely she agreed with what we were doing. I asked if she thought she'd be able to join us in a demonstration in Times Square.

"Oh, God, Alan," she said gently, "I've been marching all my life."

It hadn't occurred to me that my deeply felt cause would be one more lean on her good nature, already heavily weighted with them. I told her I understood and went down the hall to Beah Richards's dressing room.

In **Purlie,** Beah played the woman who had raised Charley. As an actor, I was learning from her every night onstage, and I would have been glad if I **had** been raised by someone with her deep understanding of humanity. She was in her forties then, and in spite of the lack of opportunity for black actors, she had become extraordinarily good at her art. I truly admired her, and I wasn't prepared for her reaction.

She listened until I finished talking, then said in a low tone that contained more concentrated fury than I had ever heard before, "I don't care if they destroy themselves with these bombs. They've brought this on themselves. I don't care if they vaporize one another and their eyes melt and run down their cheeks."

I stood still, not knowing what to say. I loved this woman, and I knew she had affection for me, but I had inadvertently opened a wound, and I regretted it. This was a time when actual bombings were more real to her as a black woman than the mere threat of nuclear war could be to me. She had lived with the bombing of black churches in the South. It wasn't hypothetical. People were dying.

Beah finally did come and walk with us. It was a cold winter night, and after the show, we gathered in Times Square and walked in a circle in the snow for about fifteen minutes. We had notified the press, but of course no one was there to watch us, and the circle of footprints we left in the snow melted away the next day along with any effect we might have had on anybody at all, other than ourselves.

Getting drunk on the desire to do something didn't mean I was accomplishing anything, but that was something I didn't understand until I saw someone else drink from that cup. A few months later, there was a large gathering of hundreds of people in Times Square, calling for a test ban treaty. I wasn't able to go because Arlene was

51

working and I stayed home with our children. But an actor friend had gone to Times Square and came to our apartment an hour later. He was shaking with adrenaline.

"You won't believe this," he said. "You won't fucking believe this." He was carrying his fifteen-month-old son, who looked confused and scared. "They charged us," my friend said. "The police charged us. With horses! Can you believe that? We had children there."

I asked him why he'd brought his child to a street demonstration. He said he wanted him to be part of a historic moment. Something he could be proud of when he grew up. "But there's always a chance the cops will overreact," I said. "Weren't you putting him in danger?"

"I didn't think they'd charge us with horses! Why would they do a thing like that?" He shook with anger and expressed amazement for another fifteen minutes.

We were all sincere and passionate, but I saw the difference between dabblers like us and a true force for change the day Martin Luther King came to the theater. **Purlie Victorious** was celebrating its hundredth performance, and he came down to the basement of the theater and had his picture taken with the cast. When I shook hands with him, the look in his eyes was unforgettable. There was an alertness I had never seen before in anyone's eyes, almost a cold stare. There was a feeling of trauma about his gaze, of looking into the distance without seeing, yet you felt he could see through you. These eyes were ready for anything: victory, defeat, death, wherever his walk would take him. You could see how the focus in those eyes could lead marches that changed lives.

Meanwhile, I was still walking in circles, the way I had in Times Square that snowy night. In the little town in New Jersey where Arlene and I lived, we picketed an apartment house that discriminated against black people. It's possible we shamed them into changing their policy, but I never knew for sure. We would turn out for demonstrations more in frustration than in hope. A year after King was assassinated, a call went out for a demonstration to mark the anniversary of his death. Those of us who had picketed together stood in silence with bowed heads in an intersection in downtown Hackensack, and then we sang "We Shall Overcome." Again, there was no one in the street but us and a few cops who were assigned to keep the peace. There was no chance that the peace was in danger of being disturbed. The cops looked at their watches and glanced at one another, shaking their heads. As I looked over at them, I felt they were a little given to smirking. But on the way home, I thought it over. What were we achieving by standing on an empty street, holding hands and singing? All it did was make us feel good. I wondered if I was accomplishing anything or just playing in the street.

I got the answer to that a couple of years later, while I was having lunch with an old friend. Bert Convy had started in the theater around the same time I had. I had known him a long time, but he casually told me a story I hadn't heard before, and it made me put down my fork and listen. A stillness came over me, the kind that hits you when you hear something that goes to the core of who you think you are. I had never thought of Bert as a political hero. He had played Perchik in **Fiddler on the Roof**; he had gone on to a career as an actor in films, a host of game shows, and an affable raconteur on the **Tonight** show. To most of us, he was a cheerful guy, skating nimbly over the surface of show business. But as he told me his story, I realized that in 1968 he had performed a small but dangerous act of courage.

That year, in frustration over events they couldn't control, people were increasingly taking to the streets. Sometimes, frustrated themselves and occasionally goaded, the cops didn't just stand around looking at their watches. Bert was there in Chicago the night they exploded. He had been working in the presidential campaign and had been sent as a delegate from New York to the Democratic convention. From his hotel room, he could see the anger growing in the street below. The crowd and the cops took turns surging toward each other, and at one point the cops began attacking the crowd with their clubs. The only escape for some demonstrators was through the doors of the hotel and into the lobby. The cops chased after them into the building, grabbing some and dragging them back into the street and into police wagons. Some demonstrators managed to make it upstairs, where Bert and other delegates let them into their rooms. Several of the young men had faces streaming with blood that Bert and his friends sopped up with hotel towels. They watched through the windows at the mayhem in the street below and saw the police getting ready to enter the hotel again. Within minutes, the police were banging on doors, demanding entry. They burst into Bert's room, started hitting the demonstrators, and pulled them, some by the hair, out of the room.

Bert was angry and upset at the violence and

what he felt was unlawful entry into his room. Having seen the kids roughed up in the hotel, he was afraid of what would happen to them at the station house. He got on the phone and found out where they were being taken. He put on his jacket and tie and went downstairs, threading his way through a violent crowd, and headed for the police station. The jacket and tie were a form of dressing for the part. When he got to the station, he identified himself as the lawyer for the demonstrators and demanded their release. The police wanted to know what law firm he was with. He said he was a lawyer from New York and wasn't going to wait until morning to verify the fact that he was a lawyer; they had violated the civil rights of his clients, and he wanted them released immediately. The audacity of his demands and the authority he was able to summon as an actor put enough pressure on the police that night for Bert to get seventeen people released.

When Bert finished his story, which he told simply and without self-aggrandizement, I was moved by his courage. Having just seen people beaten by the police, he had walked into a station house and pretended he was an officer of the court. He could have been thrown in jail himself. Years later, Bert died of a brain tumor after a long and humbling illness, and I thought that the legacy he left behind was not the lighthearted performances that many people knew him for, but the instantaneous bravery he had shown that night. Without thinking, he had stepped into danger to help people he knew nothing about, except that they were in trouble. I had done what I could in those days, but compared with Bert, I felt I **had** been at play in the streets.

I wanted to point the kids at Emerson toward something that could stir them to meaningful action, and I guess to point myself in the same direction.

It seems to me that your life will have meaning when you can give meaning to it. And not until then. Because no one else will give meaning to your life. There isn't a job or a title or a degree that has meaning in itself. The world will go stumbling on without you no matter how high your office. And there isn't any liquor that will give meaning to your life, or any drug, or any type of sexual congress, either. Not for long, anyway.

I'd like to suggest to you, just in case you haven't done it lately, that this would

be a good time to find out what your values are, and then figure out how you're going to be able to live by them. Knowing what you care about and then devoting yourself to it is just about the only way you're going to be able to have a sense of purpose in your life.

There was a day in my youth when I suddenly realized I had values. I had been acting on Broadway in **The Apple Tree** for a few months when my agent urged me to leave the show long enough to shoot a movie called **The Extraordinary Seaman.** I was still in my twenties, but I had clear ideas about what I thought was good material, and I thought this script was terrible. But my agent insisted; it would be good for my career, she said.

I couldn't understand how being in a lousy movie would be a career booster, and besides, the producer of **The Apple Tree** wanted fifty thousand dollars to let me out of the play for the three months it would take to shoot this pathetic thing.

"That was what Richard Burton paid to get out of **Camelot** in order to do **Cleopatra,**" I told my agent. "Richard **Burton.** People actually knew who he was." Arlene and I had nothing in the bank, and we would have to go into debt to make the payment.

This, I'm sorry to say, was not the moment where I found out I had values. I borrowed money to make a movie I didn't believe in. When I got back to New York, though, my agent called and said excitedly that she'd found a way to wipe out the debt. She had lined up a cigarette commercial that would pay me exactly fifty thousand dollars. This was when the values kicked in.

"No. Thanks," I said, "I'm not interested."

She was shocked. Why would I turn down fifty thousand dollars when I was exactly fifty thousand in debt?

"Well," I said, "because I don't want to take money so people can get cancer."

She thought that was a strange line of reasoning. I wasn't giving people cancer—I was collecting fifty thousand for a day's work. To be fair, this was a time when cigarettes were advertised on television and the surgeon general's warning was not yet on the package. If you wanted, you could tell yourself you were simply in step with everyone else. But in reality, we all knew cigarettes were killers. I said no again and hung up.

When I got off the phone, I realized that there were some things I valued more than others. And because of that, there was nothing hard about the choice. I hadn't faced down the Chicago police and made them hand over the bloody kids, the way Bert had. I had simply said "no thanks" to poisoning people. But I was acting, finally, on what I had suggested to the mayor of Burbank: that the people who can change things are right in this room. I realized, though, that finding out what you value isn't always that easy.

It can be surprising when you try to rank your values. Ask yourself what's the most important thing in the world to you. Your family? Your work? Your money? Your country? Getting to heaven? Sex? Dope? (Thanks, but I don't need a show of hands on this.)

When you come up with an answer to that . . . ask yourself how much time you actually spend on your number one value and how much time you spend on what you thought was number five . . . or number ten. What, in fact, is the thing you value most?

This will matter, regardless of what business you go into. When you sell a product that you know will fall apart in a few months. . . . When you sell the sizzle and you know there's no steak. . . . When you take the money and run. . . . When you write an article or a political speech or a television show that excites and titillates but doesn't lead to understanding and insight. . . . When you're all style and no substance . . . then you might as well be tossing poison into the reservoir we all drink from.

Suppose somebody offered you fifty dollars to throw a little poison in the reservoir? "Look," he says, "it's just a little poison. How much harm can it do?" What would you take to throw just a little poison in the reservoir? Fifty dollars? A hundred dollars? Ten thousand dollars? How about a half million with stock options and a Christmas bonus?

It may be "just a little," but if everyone's little bit of poison combines with everyone else's . . . then together we're tampering dangerously with the moral ecology.

Times have changed since the sixties. In those days, we were all out on the streets. We were impatient and passionate, and the depth of our caring was matched by the flamboyance of our gestures. But you've come in out of the street. They say you're thinking more about your own careers now than about marching.

If that's true, the funny thing is that it's possible that you can do more to change things than anyone could in the sixties. If you can put a high value on decency; if you can put a high value on excellence—and on family—if you can love the people you share your lives with, and if you don't shortchange them for a few bucks; if you can love the work you do; if you can give full measure to the people who pay you for your work; if you can try not to lie, try not to cheat, try to do good just by doing well whatever you do . . .

Then you will have made a revolution.

I stepped back from the microphone and went to my chair. I'd managed to say what I meant. As I sat there, half listening to the other speakers, the action on the East River went into slow motion and the tin can reversed its course. The wound in the scalp closed, and the girl on the running board smiled. Even the mayor of Burbank smiled.

Chapter 4

Bandages and Badinage

I walked out onto a grassy field on the Upper West Side of Manhattan, looked at the expectant faces of the young doctors and their parents, and tried to establish my noncredentials right away.

> Ever since they announced that an actor had been invited to speak at this commencement, people have been wondering—why get someone who only plays a doctor when you could get a real one?

This had been a tough one. I had been asked to speak to the graduating class of the Columbia University College of Physicians and Surgeons, one of the most respected medical colleges in the country. Karen Kosovsky, a young friend of our family, was graduating that day, and I wanted to accept, but the invitation scared me. In what way could I possibly speak from my own experience to medical students? The closest I had come to a personal experience with doctoring had been trying to wash the fake blood off my underwear when it soaked through my fatigues on M*A*S*H. I worried that even showing up that day would make it seem that I was an actor who actually believed he was the doctor he played. I couldn't think of an angle to come in on, and I thought I ought to turn it down. But I couldn't disappoint Karen, and I said yes. As the day came closer when I'd have to get up and speak, I wondered what use I could be to young doctors.

Maybe the school has done everything it could to show you how to be doctors, and in a moment of desperation they've brought in someone who can show you how to act like one. I'm certainly not a doctor. In the first place, I'm not a great

fan of blood. I don't mind people's having it, I just don't enjoy seeing them wear it. And I've yet to see a real operation, because the mere smell of a hospital reminds me of a previous appointment.

I had heard too many stories of medical students fainting at autopsies for me to be able to watch actual surgery. And the idea of seeing surgeons piercing living people with a knife and spreading their ribs apart so they could stick their hands inside their warm, personal interiors just didn't seem like fun. I had done my research for Hawkeye in books rather than operating rooms. But as hard as it was to believe, at some point in the eleven years M*A*S*H was on the air, in some people's **minds,** I had become a doctor.

Once, in the middle of the night, our friend Esther's husband fell down in the bathroom a few steps from their bed, and, hearing the thump, she woke and went to him. He was facedown, unconscious, blood spreading from his head onto the white tiles. As she tried frantically to revive him, she mentally listed all the people she could call for help. And the first person she thought of was **me.** I was what came to mind when there was blood on the floor.

Fortunately, she also came up with a couple of other people who were actually doctors, and one of them came to the house and tended to her husband. When she told us about it the next day, I was astonished that I was at the top of her list. "What did you think I could do?" I asked her. "Run over and tell him a couple of jokes?" We laughed about it, but I realized how easy it is to let playacting substitute for reality. It was a mistake I didn't want to make myself when I talked to these brand-new doctors.

My knowledge of anatomy resides in the clear understanding that the hipbone is connected to the legbone. I am not a doctor. But you've asked me here, and all in all I think you made a wonderful choice. That's because I probably first came to your attention through a character on television that I've played and helped write for the past seven years: a surgeon called Hawkeye Pierce. He's a remarkable person, and if you've chosen somehow to associate his character with your graduation from medical school, then I find that very heartening. Because I think it means that you're reaching out toward a humane kind of doctoring. And toward a real kind of doctor. We didn't make him up. He really lived as several doctors who struggled to preserve life twenty-five years ago during the Korean War.

It was surprising, actually, how many people had come up to me and told me they knew the actual doctor Hawkeye was based on; if they had, there would have been twenty-five or thirty Hawkeyes. There couldn't have been that many. But he seemed so real to people, they believed they'd actually known him.

There's something especially engaging about him because he's based on real doctors. He has a sense of humor and yet he's serious. He's impertinent and yet he has feeling. He's human enough to make mistakes and yet he hates death enough to push himself past his own limits to save lives. In many ways, he's the doctor patients want and doctors want to be. But he's not an idealization. Finding himself in a war, he's sometimes angry, sometimes cynical, sometimes a little nuts. He's not a magician who can come up with an instant cure without sweating and ruining his makeup. He knows he might fail. Not a god, he walks gingerly on the edge of disaster—alive to his own mortality.

There was, in fact, a complexity to Hawkeye's character that wasn't easy for me to understand at first. As actors, we pretty much had only our imaginations to rely on when we began the show. Somehow we had to take on the look and feel of people who had gone through years of grueling training and then months of combat surgery. Gene Reynolds, who produced the early years of the show, knew we couldn't be expected to come up with all this out of pure imagination and had a medical adviser on the set when we shot the first episode.

In one of the opening scenes, we were up on the helipad, shielding our eyes as the helicopter landed, raising a cloud of dust. I ran over to it, crouching under the spinning blades—not so much because they were low, but because I had never been that close to a helicopter before and I didn't want to get my head whipped off. I called out directions to the orderlies as they lifted a wounded man off the chopper and carried his stretcher to a jeep. I jogged beside him, concerned, checking him out as we ran. Dr. Walter Dishell, our medical adviser, was watching us from behind the camera.

We did a couple of takes, and then Walter came over to me. "You know what? Don't look so compassionate," he said. "You've done this hundreds of times. Just get the job done." I looked at the fake blood on my patient. **How can I just take that in stride?** I thought. Walter looked at me with some sympathy, but he was firm about it. "You've seen this over and over," he said.

In the next take, I took my foot off the empathy pedal and the scene went better. Hawkeye's concern for the patient had more power when it was more visible in his actions than on his sleeve.

If this image of that very human, very caring doctor is attractive to you—if it's ever touched you for a moment as something to reach for in your own life— then I'm here to cheer you on. Do it, go for it. Be skilled, be learned, be aware of the dignity of your calling . . . but please don't ever lose sight of your own simple humanity.

You've spent years in a grueling effort to understand the structure and processes

of human life. It's required the knowledge of complexities within complexities. You have skills that have been hard to acquire. I only ask one thing of you: Possess your skills, but don't be possessed by them.

I was talking about how hard it can be to deal with people in a crisis. It's more comfortable to retreat to cool skills and expertise. But the right mix of cool and warm isn't easy to achieve. Even for those of us who were just **playing** doctors, finding the right mix was at the center of what we had to learn to do on **M*A*S*H**. The show would be serious and funny. There would be light moments and dark. Empathy mixed with shenanigans. The real doctors we were playing cared about their patients, of course, yet when they operated on them, they would often be joking with one another. I was surprised when I first heard this about surgeons, but then I realized that they would have to take the pressure off themselves in some way. And in fact, that's what happened to us as we played those surgeons. After twelve or fourteen hours of shooting in the operating room, under pressure that scrambled our brains, we started playing practical jokes on one another. At the end of a take, anyone who had been especially sincere or heartfelt during the shot would get pelted with wads of rolled-up surgical tape as soon as we heard the word "Cut!" Or we would sneak up behind an actor and see how many surgical instruments could be clamped to the back of his surgical gown before he noticed he was dragging a half pound of metal behind him.

So I began to see a paradox both in doctoring and in acting: the need to be empathetic and coolheaded at the same time. You had to have some distance from it, but not too much. We had to be precise in our work; words and motions had to be exact. You needed to get your hand into a sticky surgical glove in exactly the time it took to speak some complicated medical talk. Sometimes the comic business needed split-second timing. Yet if there was no simple authenticity about it, it would look mechanical. To keep technique from dominating us, we cut through it with playfulness. We were a little like the surgeons in this: For the patients' well-being, we layered them in bandages; but for our own well-being, we laid on the badinage.

As I talked to the young doctors graduating from Columbia P&S, I was struck by this tension between technical skill and the human connection and how sometimes they could be at odds with each other.

> You've had to toughen yourself to death.
> From your first autopsy when you may
> have been sick or cried or just been numb,
> you've had to inure yourself to death in
> order to be useful to the living. But I hope
> in the process you haven't done too good a
> job in burying that part of you that hurts
> and is afraid.
>
> I know what it's like to be absorbed in
> technique. When I write for M*A*S*H, I'm
> always writing about people with what I
> hope is compassion and feeling. Yet one day
> I found myself talking to someone who was
> in a real crisis, in real pain, and I remember
> thinking, This would make a great story.
>
> Becoming set apart—becoming your
> skill—can make it tough to face your
> feelings, and you get left out of the loop.

I was unqualified to talk to them about medicine. But I **was** an expert in one area of medicine: I had been a **patient.** This was an expertise from which I could speak to young doctors from the heart.

With all your study, you can name all the bones in my body. You can read my X-rays like a telegram. But can you read my involuntary muscles? Can you see the fear and uncertainty in my face?

If I tell you where it hurts, can you hear in my voice where I ache?

I show you my body, but I bring you my person. Can you see me through your reading glasses?

Will you tell me what you're planning on doing to me, and in words I can understand?

Will you tell me when you don't know what to do? Can you face your own fear, your own uncertainty? When in doubt, can you call in help?

Even if, in time, you don't deal directly with patients—if you're in research, administration, if you write—no matter what you do—eventually there is always going to be a patient at the other end of your decisions.

Will you care more about the case than the person? ("Nurse, have the gastric ulcer come in at three." . . . "How's the fractured femur in room 208?")

You'll know you're in trouble if you find yourself wishing they would mail you their liver in a plain brown envelope.

Where does money come on your list? Will it be the standard against which you reckon your success?

I didn't know then that one day medicine in our country would be run by accountants and that actual doctors would have little chance of making any money—unless they ran an HMO. If they did, there would be a special waiting room for them in the outer office of heaven, where they would sit forever.

Where will your family come on your list? How many days and nights, weeks and months, will you separate yourself from them, buried in your work, before you realize that you removed yourself from an important part of your life?

And if you're a male doctor, how will you relate to women? Women as patients, as nurses, as fellow doctors—and later as students. Will you be able to respect your patient's right to know and make decisions about her own body? Will you see nurses as colleagues—or as handmaidens? I hope you men will work to grant the same dignity to your female colleagues that you yourselves enjoy.

And if you're a female doctor, I hope you'll be aware that you didn't get where you are all by yourself. You've had to work hard, but you're sitting where you are right now in part because way back in 1848 in Seneca Falls, women you never knew began insisting you had the right to sit there. Just as they helped a generation they would never see, I urge you to work for the day when your daughters and their daughters will be called not "a woman doctor" or "my doctor, who's a woman," but simply "my doctor."

When you think about it, there isn't an area of your work that won't be affected by what you decide to place a high value on and what you decide doesn't count.

Well, that's my prescription. I've given you kind of a big pill to swallow, but I think it'll make you feel better.

I thank you for taking on the enormous responsibility of caring for other people's lives and for having the strength to have made it to this day. I don't know how you've managed to learn it all. But there is one more thing you can learn about the body that only a nondoctor would tell you, and I hope you'll always remember it:

The head bone is connected to the heart bone—don't let them come apart.

Many years later, a young woman came up to me in an airport and told me she had been there that day in the graduating class. She said that for a long time she had carried a copy of the talk around with her to remind herself of the kind of doctor she wanted to be. I was moved by the thought that someone had actually taken my words to heart. And it wasn't until then that I got the real message of what I'd said that day: how much more alive you can feel—even a sense of purpose—knowing there are real lives at the other end of your ministrations, or your art, or your talk, or even your jokes.

Chapter 5

The Talking and the Doing of It

You could hear them falling from the trees and thudding onto the ground or hitting the shoulders of the people listening to the commencement speakers. They were locusts: long, green, swarming grasshoppers. It was 1982, and since we assumed they were seventeen-year locusts, we felt they hadn't been out in the real world like this since 1965, which might account for their curiosity as they climbed up people's legs or crawled around on their laps while the talks went on.

It was hard to think of anything but bugs that day. Elie Wiesel was there to receive an honorary doctorate from Kenyon College, as I was. We ran into each other a couple of decades later, and the first thing he said was, "Remember the locusts?" I gave the commencement talk, but all I remember of it now was a sea of faces registering revulsion and disgust.

They were probably reacting to the green things on their legs and not to my talk, but when I look again at the things I said—a litany of troubles that was the state of our world then—it makes me a little sad.

I cataloged things the graduates could do to make the world better, but it was really a list of all the ways we had screwed things up for them. I hadn't done any special research; I got all my depressing information from the daily newspapers. When I look back now and imagine that sunny day twenty-five years ago when my daughter Elizabeth was graduating from Kenyon College with hope in her heart and a chuckle in her throat, I notice that, in fact, it wasn't sunny. It was gloomy and gray; the world had been mangled, and on top of that, locusts were falling out of the trees onto our heads. There aren't any good old days. On that day, though, she did have hope and a chuckle.

It was something she always had. Not long

after she was born, the doctor said her feet were turned in a little. It wasn't serious, he said. Casts for two or three months would straighten them out. At first, we were brought down by the sight of her small legs heavy with the plaster that encased them. But within a few days, we noticed she had invented a game. She knocked the casts together and laughed at the sound they made. She had turned them into a giant pair of castanets. She would grin up at us from her crib and slam the casts together, laughing toothlessly. Her laughter cheered us, as it would time after time from then on.

As she got older, her wit sharpened to a fine point. There was a running joke in the family, promoted usually by Elizabeth, about my nose, which the children regarded as unusually long. Once, on a cold day when she was eight, I announced that the end of my nose was freezing. "Sure," she said, "the circulation can't get out that far." I told my friends how funny she was and offered her twenty-five cents for every funny line she or her sisters submitted to me for a television series I was writing. If I used the line, I would give them a dollar. It wasn't that I was cheap; I just wanted to help them know the value of money. This led to some frugality on their part, but mostly to a new line of jokes about how cheap I was.

But now something new was happening. The little kid who went to sleep laughing while I sat at her bedside was graduating from college. And I was at the podium, looking for words that could catch this transition just long enough to make sense of it.

It seems hard to believe that you grew from that little baby . . . into a friend of mine. From my child to my equal.

I don't know about everyone's mom and dad today, but I know that for me—as glad as I am for you, as much as I feel this sense of pride and relief and accomplishment— that's how nervous, anxious, and edgy I am about this whole thing.

I was talking to my daughter from my heart to hers, but I felt I had to make it a public talk, and I headed off on a commencement riff about the state of the world. I should have kept it personal.

What bothers me is not just letting you go. It's the world you'll be going into that scares me. What kind of place have we

made ready for you? And how will you cope with it? Dirty water, dirty air, racism, sexism, unemployment, inflation, crime in places high and low, war and rumors of war: It's a real utopia.

We're leaving you with a government that solves these problems in an oddly creative way. "Why think of them as problems?" they seem to be saying. "Let all the problems be solutions for one another." A couple of months ago, the president suggested that the unemployment figures would be much lower if we just stopped counting so many women among the unemployed.

You may feel that working on all this will take forever. But, actually, all these problems can be wiped out in five minutes, because we're also leaving you the nuclear bomb. This is the ultimate problem solver, and Washington has been thinking about it.

They have a department in Washington called the Federal Emergency Management Agency, whose job it is to prepare America for the effects of a nuclear war. The head of this agency has been quoted as saying that after a nuclear war, "whatever the losses in food and manufacturing, they will be balanced by losses in population." So one problem solves another.

FEMA was only three years old in 1982, and I hadn't heard much about it. It wasn't as far removed from reality as it would be after Hurricane Katrina, but they were already operating from another planet.

The agency says it hopes to keep American deaths down to only forty-five million in a nuclear war, and they have stashed away seventy-five thousand pounds of opium in secret locations to ease the suffering of those who survive the firestorm.

By the way, I'm not making any of this up. We're giving you a world that runs like clockwork. And the clock it runs like is a cuckoo clock.

I couldn't do much about the bomb. I'm sorry. I started working for a treaty to ban nuclear tests almost twenty years ago, when you were very small. But instead of things getting better, they've got worse.

Scientists have calculated that the three

hundred million dollars it took to wipe out smallpox in the last decade are equal to five hours of the military budget.

Eighty percent of the world's illness is caused by contaminated water, yet the cost of a sanitary global water supply is equal to three weeks of the arms race.

I know that today these words sound like the ravings of a naïve Hollywood liberal, but in a way, I can't help it. I grew up in an age when this kind of woolly thinking was common. Take, for instance, this stinging denunciation of war and the preparations for war by a typical lefty of my youth:

"Every gun that is made, every warship launched, every rocket fired, signifies, in the final sense, a theft from those who hunger and are not fed, those who are cold and not clothed. This world in arms is not spending money alone. It is spending the sweat of its laborers, the genius of its scientists, the hopes of its children. This is not a way of life at all in any true sense. Under the cloud of threatening war, it is humanity hanging from a cross of iron."

These words, which today might seem dangerously close to undermining our national defense, were spoken in 1953 by President Dwight D. Eisenhower.

I wanted to speak to Elizabeth's hope and cheerfulness, but there were a string of mournful events fresh in my mind that day, and I couldn't keep away from them. I had just spent almost ten years campaigning for the Equal Rights Amendment. Scenes from those years still flashed in my mind. Eleanor Smeal and I pulling up to a church in Oklahoma, running in, and speaking to a crowd that surged and swayed with energy. Working with dignified, graceful Betty Ford, announcing a countdown campaign in the last year we had to get it ratified. Standing with Arlene and our daughters in Lafayette Park outside the White House, urging a crowd of a thousand people to not give up. But here was a time limit on ratification. Time had almost run out in 1979 when Congress voted for an extension. Now, in May 1982, if the amendment wasn't ratified by three more states within a few weeks, it would not become part of the Constitution, and there was no chance for that to happen.

I wanted to give you a world that respected you as a woman as much as it did me as a man. I wanted the pledge of

that respect engraved in our Constitution. But, unless a miracle happens within the next thirty-seven days, you're not going to get it. You'll pay the same taxes as a man, Congress can send you to war, just like a man, but you won't be guaranteed equality of rights under the law. Not this year, and not next year, and maybe not for the rest of this century.

While we were campaigning for the amendment, I heard three fears expressed by opponents with surprising frequency. One was that under the ERA men and women would have to share the same bathrooms. This seems ludicrous now, but people actually expressed this concern on the floor in a number of state assemblies. Another was the worry that women would be forced to fight in the military alongside men, and the third was that states would be forced to allow same-sex marriages. Legal scholars said repeatedly that whether or not these outcomes were desirable, none of them would be mandated by the amendment. But the fears won the day, and the amendment wasn't ratified.

Our culture changed anyway. Without the amendment, we now have men and women using the same bathrooms (sometimes, in college dorms, the same showers), we have women fighting and dying alongside men in combat zones, and in some states, there are same-sex marriages. But women and men still aren't guaranteed equality under the Constitution.

There always had been plenty wrong with the world, of course, and there probably always would be. The hope for my daughter was that she would be strong enough to survive in it.

If there's one urgent thought I want to leave in your ear in this parting hug—it's that I want you to be strong. I don't mean hard and brittle. The tree that won't bend with the storm will snap in two. I hope you'll flex and give and then stand straight again with your roots where they ought to be.

And being strong doesn't mean having all the answers. Even when you're in charge of something, don't be afraid not to know exactly what you're doing. Ask questions. Some people may look at you funny, worried at your hesitation. They're only showing their own frailty. I've known some strong people, and they weren't afraid to

hold their uncertain ground while they searched for a solution.

It takes courage to be creative. And we're going to need your creativity or we're done for. And I hope you'll give other people a chance to be uncertainly creative, too. Someone else may be able to contribute one idea that will solve one of the insurmountable problems we're handing you, even though that person may be totally wrong about everything else.

Steer clear of ideology. Like jargon, it can be a substitute for thought. The lure of the simple solution can lead to handing over your life to people who make the trains run on time—but who take away your freedom to go where you want on those trains.

Be open to change, and take risks— that's the adventure and the art of life. Find the bridge between constancy and experiment. Be flexible, but principled. Be a dissenter, but patriotic. Be disciplined, but improvise.

Freud said, "Health is the ability to work and to love." Add a third: Be able to play. Be playful about the most serious things in your life; you'll enjoy them more and have them longer. Playfulness is a sudden shift of vision—a kind of affectionate dissent. It brings you closer to what you love.

Be flexible about your dreams. Say hello to change. I had an economics teacher in college, Mr. Partlan, who said, "Don't be afraid to change your mind about your career. You can keep changing till you're forty." I know people who are changing in their sixties. Be supple. Be loose. Life is one surprise after another.

College has been like climbing a mountain. You had to persevere, stretch your reach, endure the loneliness of the midnight book. And now you're at the summit—and what do you see in front of you? More mountains. The only thing you can be sure of is that there will always be more mountains.

But I know you'll be okay. Your laughter, your honesty, your youthful energy and optimism—that makes me know that life is possible.

Because you can wrap your brain
around a tough idea, because you can learn
an art—tell a joke, play the piano—
because you can laugh with a lusty
abandon: Because of simple things like
these, I know that nature will survive.

I wish I had a better world to give
you. But maybe we can work on one
together now.

So long, my child. Hello, my friend.

Elizabeth graduated, and we took off on a
trip together. Arlene had come up with an anti-
dote for the time I had been away from our
daughters while I worked in California. As soon
as she graduated, each daughter could choose a
trip anywhere in the world, and she and I would
go there together. Eve chose Greece, Beatrice
chose China, and Elizabeth decided on a trip on
the **Orient Express** from Paris to Venice, then
Salzburg and Vienna.

It didn't start out as the trip of our dreams—
or, at least, not mine. We waited at the train station in Paris, with our bags splayed out on the
floor, listening for the announcement to board
the train. Nothing came over the speakers. We

waited an hour and still nothing. Finally, with a half hour to go, I left Elizabeth to watch the bags while I went to see the stationmaster.

"**Non,**" he said, "**le train est parti.**"

I had spent my junior year of college in Paris, and unfortunately, I had no trouble understanding him.

"The train couldn't have left," I told him in impeccably accented hysteria. "My daughter and I have tickets for that train."

"No, no," he said, using two **no**'s where one would have been superfluous, if not offensive. "They left three hours early. They notified all their customers."

"They didn't notify me."

"Possibly you bought your ticket in America."

"I did."

"Perhaps it's that." This was followed by a shrug described either as Gallic or sadistic, depending on how much you're willing to forgive the French in exchange for Château Lafite.

"No, no, no," I said, seeing his two **no**'s and raising him one. "It is necessary that we get on that train. This is a very important trip for my daughter. It is absolutely necessary that we get on that train."

"Mais, le train est parti."

I was in no mood for French logic. "My daughter will be desolated. This is not possible."

"Well, you might try getting on the **Blue Train,** which hasn't left yet. It runs much faster than the **Orient Express.** If you get off in Dijon, you can flag down the **Orient Express** when it passes through."

Flag down the **Orient Express.** How was I supposed to do that?

"Just go to the stationmaster and tell him you have to stop the **Orient Express.**"

It was **absolument** absurd that a stationmaster in Dijon would stop a train just because I told him to, but I thought of Elizabeth, waiting beside the bags.

"All right, but I want you to put that in writing. 'To the stationmaster of Dijon: I authorize you to stop the **Orient Express.**' And sign it 'the Stationmaster of Paris.'"

"That's not necessary."

"It is absolutely necessary."

"If you don't leave now, you're going to miss the **Blue Train.**"

"Not without written authorization."

"I have nothing to write on."

He was driving me crazy. A stationmaster without a letterhead. How could the man exist in Paris without official paper?

"Here, write on this." From the top of a filing cabinet, I grabbed a brown paper bag with a couple of grease stains on it from his lunch. He took the bag from me with an expression that was a precisely calculated mix of disdain and pity and wrote what I dictated in a nice, florid hand. I insisted he sign it "the Paris Stationmaster." I thanked him and left.

I grabbed up Elizabeth and the bags, and we ran for **le Train Bleu.** There were no seats left, and we stood all the way to Dijon while a group of young sailors blew smoke at us that they sucked from their Gauloises.

Finally, at two in the morning, we were the only people to get off the train in Dijon. The place was deserted, and as the **Blue Train** pulled away into the black night, we saw a tiny shack at the end of the platform with a dim light burning in the window. I walked down to it and knocked on the door. It opened just a crack.

"**Oui?**"

"Good evening. It will be necessary to stop the **Orient Express.**"

"No. The **Orient Express** does not stop in Dijon."

"Tonight, it is necessary that it stop. We have tickets."

"I cannot stop the **Orient Express.**"

"Really?" I pulled out the brown paper bag. "Read this!"

He looked as if I had offered him a rodent. "What's that?"

"That is official authorization from the Paris stationmaster. The **Paris** stationmaster. We must stop that train."

He took the bag from me and read it carefully. "You got this from the Paris stationmaster?"

"That's right. In Paris." I felt I couldn't say the word **Paris** too many times.

Silently, he nodded. "All right, I'll stop it."

A few minutes later, the **Orient Express** pulled to a halt and some disgruntled train workers got off, wanting to know what the problem was. I showed them our tickets and told them we wanted to be taken to our compartments. Well, they said, the compartments have to be made up. It will take a while.

I was in no mood for delays. I had power now. I had stopped the **Orient Express** with a paper bag. I didn't know the official title of the person in charge, but I said, "**Je veux voir le directeur du train!**" instinctively certain that this was the way to say it.

They looked puzzled. "The **director** of the train? Who is that?"

"The chief. The master. The captain."

"He's asleep."

And here, I rose to my full height. "**Pourquoi doit-il dormir**," I said, "**pendant que moi, je marche dans la rue?**" (Why should he sleep, while I walk in the street?) My fifteen months in France had been a painstaking preparation for this one grand turn of phrase, which they tried to dismiss as sounding idiotic.

"Please get on board. We can't stay all night in Dijon."

They could pretend I hadn't scored on them, but I ushered Elizabeth onto the train with the clear knowledge I had beaten them in their own language.

Once on the train, the trip didn't improve. The train must have been built a hundred years earlier, and the bed was designed for people who were a foot shorter than me. I slept with my knees up near my chin.

All the while, Elizabeth was enjoying this

with a delighted, mischievous smile. Her playfulness didn't seem to have a bottom to it. There was one place she had to visit in Vienna: the Prater. This, she said, was an amusement park with spectacular rides. There was nothing like it in the world. I was there to do anything she wanted, and we went. It turned out that she wanted us to go on a ride that barreled through space at about ninety miles an hour, doing loops and finally plummeting dizzyingly toward the earth. I didn't think I was interested.

"Oh, come on. Don't be a fogy."

Reluctantly, I got behind her on the ride, and the gondola started its slow climb to the top. **Well, it's not so bad,** I thought as we leveled off at the summit. Then the front end of the gondola tipped down, and I realized we were going to die. We plummeted—and then, with no warning, we suddenly rose up toward the sky again. My face smashed into the back of Elizabeth's head, and my nose went numb. "Isn't this great?" she said.

We twisted to the right, then the left, then we dove, climbed again, then headed straight for the earth. We were both screaming like chimpanzees. Finally the ride came to a halt. Every muscle in my body was trembling.

Elizabeth turned and looked at me with a grin. "Let's go again."

When we got home from our trip, Elizabeth began working on a career as an actress. She studied, she went to auditions, and she got an occasional acting job. Little by little, though, she began to realize that she didn't enjoy acting as much as she thought she would. One night she worked on a movie, playing a cop with just a line or two. She had to run to a corpse and say something procedural. But after several takes, her thighs ached. She was hungry and cold. And there wasn't much acting involved. She began to realize that even when she worked she didn't enjoy it that much. She'd been wonderful in **The Four Seasons**—spontaneous and light-hearted and tearful when that was needed. She had been in the film and the short-lived television series based on the film. But now she began to think about her life in a different way.

As a sophomore at Kenyon, she had spent a semester at the National Theatre Institute school and became friends with deaf actors from the National Theatre of the Deaf. She was fascinated with sign language and the deaf community and when she decided to leave acting, she went to

graduate school in special education, and became a teacher of the deaf.

Her first student was a girl she followed
throughout her day, in a school for hearing children, translating for her in sign language. Her
joy in her student's progress made her glow. She
had gone from performing for thousands to
teaching one single person, and it couldn't have
made her feel more fulfilled. It was what I had
hoped for her in her life, and she had found the
way all by herself. She hadn't needed my words
of wisdom at her graduation.

I thought I was giving the commencement
talk that day, but the locusts gave a better one.
They left a more lasting impression. They were
the ones with the subtle, life-enhancing message.
Going about their lives, they followed the signals
inside them. When it was time to be dormant,
they took a rest. When it was time to swarm, they
swarmed all over us.

I doubt that Elizabeth remembered that I
asked her to be flexible that day and to be true to
herself. But that's what she did. Like the innocent, curious locusts, she followed her nature,
she listened to her heart. And her simple doing
of it meant more than my talking ever could.

Chapter 6

A Passion for Reason

Thomas Jefferson and I might not have become friends if we hadn't been brought together by Julann Griffin.

Julann had stuck a pin in a map, and it landed on a town in Virginia, so she sold her house, bought a farm, and moved to Palmyra, not far from Jefferson's Monticello. I always admired her courage for picking up and moving; her willingness to step out into randomness and take a walk. Past the age of sixty, she wanted to set out on a new life, to leave California, where she lived then, and she decided to stick a pin in a map. Julann is open to unconventional ideas, and she felt, I think, that her unconscious, or the spirit world, or some unseen power, would guide the pin. Whatever power it was, it didn't do too badly, because within a few months, she had an old house on a thousand acres, a pond full of fish, an old graveyard, some chickens, and a huge pig named Nancy. She loved the place and invited us to stay with her for a few days.

When we got there, Arlene and I both had bad colds. Julann went to a closet, opened a large case in which she kept homeopathic medicine, and gave us two glass vials. When we got upstairs to our room, we regarded each other with what you could call a questioning look. As I understand it, the theory behind homeopathic medicine is that you ingest a highly diluted dose of a substance that will induce the same symptoms you're suffering from, with the hope that the body will fight off all similar symptoms.

But the substance is so diluted that there isn't even a molecule of it left in the solution, just some supposed molecular memory. So what good can it do? On the other hand, how could it hurt? So we took it.

An hour later, we were dumbfounded. My cold was gone, and so was Arlene's. We told Julann with amazement that we actually felt better, but she took its efficacy so for granted that we avoided using the word **placebo.** Julann liked to experiment and invent. She once concocted an antimosquito lotion made of herbs and vodka that worked so well, we urged her to market it. She said she would, but she couldn't remember what herbs she'd used. And the vodka made the stuff too expensive. But her bent for invention made Thomas Jefferson's house, which was a few miles from her farm, one of her favorite places.

She drove us there and introduced us to Dan Jordan, who runs the place. He took us on a tour of the ingenious gimmicks in Monticello: the giant clock Jefferson had designed for the hallway, with weights that went all the way down through a hole in the floor to the basement; the cabinet that servants would fill with dishes of food in the kitchen and then swung on a hinge so they would appear magically in the dining room. Dan let me sit in a leather chair with large wings that had been designed by Jefferson. I was sure that Jefferson, who was partly deaf, had formed the wings of the chair into a parabola in order to hear conversation better. Dan said I had a pretty creative thought, which was a gracious way of saying it was just the other side of unlikely. But I clung to the idea—even after I sat in it and felt no improvement in my own poor hearing. I've always been a little more creative than necessary.

A couple of years later, Dan called and invited me to give a talk at Monticello. I certainly like hearing myself talk, but I had no idea what I'd say. "Thanks," I said, "I'm fascinated with Jefferson, but I don't think I know enough about him to give a talk." He hinted that I could just speak for a few minutes about how much I admired Jefferson. People would be glad to hear whatever I had to say. Who would these people be? I wondered. Who would be listening to me? "Oh," he said, "the board of trustees and some Jefferson scholars. A few historians."

I froze.

He was asking me to talk about Jefferson in front of historians? Wouldn't that be sort of insane?

"Sure," I said. "That sounds like fun."

I put down the phone and started making notes on what I knew about Jefferson. After a few minutes, I had a mostly blank page. But I had five months to get ready. I went to a bookstore and bought everything with Jefferson's name on the cover. I especially liked one book by Silvio Bedini that concentrated on Jefferson as a scientist. I was having a great time reading about him, but after a while, a thought crept over me like a cat's paws on your lungs just before it squeezes the life out of you. **These people have not only read this stuff, they probably wrote some of it.** How could I say anything they hadn't heard before? How could I make it worth their while to sit there while I opened and closed my mouth? This was going to be impossible. There was no way I could come up with something new or interesting.

And that was when I understood why I had agreed to talk: exactly because it terrified me.

Terrifying myself, it turns out, is one of the ways I have of feeling alive. It gives a sense of accomplishment to my life.

Nothing feels as good to me as doing something I know how to do. But if I do it too many times, it feels easy and a little slick; it loses some of its pleasure. So I have to keep looking for things that are just a little harder. This produces a feeling that's very close to accomplishment—if I can actually do it, of course. And this time, as the months went on, the pages stayed white.

I wanted to say something new, but not so new that it wasn't true. I didn't want to get overly creative, as when I sat in Jefferson's wingback chair, inventing things for him he hadn't invented himself. A few months on, I got a call from Dan, gently checking up on me. "How's it going? Can we give you any help with background material?"

"Well, I've got a lot of stuff here."

"What are you reading?"

"A lot. I like the Bedini book."

"Bedini is good. You're safe with Bedini."

His tone was cheerful, but it was becoming clear that, although the invitation was to say anything I liked about Jefferson, I wasn't supposed to say something stupid. That seemed like a good idea to me, too.

I tried one tack after another. I knew I should somehow make a personal connection to Jefferson, but what would it be? He had lived so long ago; he was a genius in so many ways. Aside from helping found a country and becoming its secretary of state, its vice president, and twice its president, he was an inventor, educator, musician, mathematician, geographer, philosopher, botanist, physicist, linguist, agronomist, archaeologist, meteorologist, paleontologist—and either he made important contributions to these fields or he **created** them. He was one of our greatest writers; he could fit the dreams of a nation into a handful of words and make them ring down through two centuries. Where, exactly, did my life intersect with his?

The months started flying by like the scene in

a 1940s movie where the pages fly off the calendar, and I was getting nowhere. Finally, I noticed I was having a recurring daydream in which I stood in front of an imposing gathering of historians on the grass in front of Monticello, and as I looked down at my speech, I saw twenty blank pages. I realized it was time to do something drastic. So I stuck a pin in a map.

I was scheduled to fly to China a month before my talk to interview scientists for **Scientific American Frontiers.** And that's where I stuck the pin. I decided that somewhere in China, someone would tell me something about Jefferson that no one had ever heard before in the States. Someone would give me such fresh insight into the man, I would come back with a thought worth listening to. China was the place.

This was, of course, nuts. But I had begun my theatrical life as an improviser, and it seemed perfectly natural to me to get my inspiration from an impossible source. "Reach into the dark and pull out the answer," we used to say. Not knowing what's coming next can be a pleasant state, if you trust it.

The difficulty is that you have to keep trusting it even when there's no evidence that it's working. I flew to China, and as the days went by,

Thomas Jefferson was nowhere to be found. I kept asking people if they had ever heard of him, and I got blank stares. What had I been thinking?

Maybe I had expected too much. I had been in love with China since the first time I went there in 1980, thinking I might be able to shoot a sequel to **The Four Seasons.** I loved the people, and I tried to teach myself the language, tripping over the tones, the way I had in glee club as a boy. In Mandarin, if you get one of four musical tones wrong, the word means something else. I took my movie to a group of filmmakers and told them in my weirdest Chinese, "I'm very happy to show you my film: **Four Seasons.**" I had the words right, but not the tones. What they heard me say was: "I'm very happy to show you my film: **Dead Chicken.**"

But I kept trying. Every night at dinner, we were given a banquet by a different committee. After a few days, I realized that this was not so much from hospitality as from their desire to have a really good meal for a change. China was still a desperately poor country.

I looked forward to these banquets. The Chinese I was meeting with laughed and ate and drank with the same joy as Italians. I would spend each day working out a couple of sentences I could say in their language to impress both them and myself. While I was delivering a particularly poetic thought in Chinese, a thin, scholarly man sitting next to Arlene leaned over to her and said somewhat wryly, "Your husband has the accent of a Tibetan monk." I took this as a compliment in spite of how they felt about Tibetan monks.

When we went there with the science show in 1995, China had become in some ways another country. Now it was Glorious to be Rich, and a lot of people in the big cities were covering themselves with glory. One of the scientists I talked to was a mathematician who ran a successful company in Hong Kong. For a half million dollars he had bought a Beijing apartment a few doors down the street from people who still rented apartments from their work units for three dollars a month. Everywhere, rising out of the dusty streets were spikes of affluence as tall buildings poked into the sky. Shanghai now used as much electricity for its neon signs as it had used twenty years earlier to light the whole city.

Everyone I met was trying to start a business. One of our science stories dealt with a lab in San Francisco that was analyzing herbs from traditional Chinese medicine to see if they actually cured anything—so I toured an herb garden. The man who ran it was very interested in showing me how valuable his herbs were.

"You see that bush over there?" he said. "Cures AIDS."

"Really." I was mildly amazed that we had never heard of it in our country.

He pointed to a plant that cured something else, and then we turned down another path. "See that plant over there? That cures AIDS, too."

By the time he pointed out the third plant that cured AIDS, I was getting testy.

"Do you have one here that **doesn't** cure AIDS?"

He seemed to miss the irony and went on to tell me I ought to think about investing in his company. "Chinese herbs are very popular," he told me. The prospect of learning anything about Jefferson was getting dimmer.

And then I met Yuan Long Ping.

We were standing in a rice paddy in Jianjiang. He was shorter than me and wiry, with the skin of a man who had spent years in the sun. His eyes looked straight into yours, and when he smiled or laughed, you joined him in it. You couldn't help it.

We rode a bus into the countryside while he tried to catch me up on all the biology I had missed while I was daydreaming in high school. He energetically crammed me full of alleles, dominant and recessive, and "characters." I couldn't get this thing about characters. Did it mean **characteristics**? Was his English in need of repair? I kept repeating what he said, but calling them "characteristics," and that's when his unique teaching style came into play. As we bumped down the country road, he got up from his seat and leaned over me. He grabbed my shirt in his skinny hands and put his face an inch from mine: "Alan. Listen to me. Try to understand: Character. **Character!**" I thought he was going to choke me.

When I got off the bus and stepped into the rice paddy, I stepped all the way into it, slipping into a ditch full of water. He had a good laugh out of that and then patiently showed me how he had transformed rice production in China, and all over Asia, with an ingenious method that involved simple tools like a rope and a beer bottle—and a deep understanding of genetics. As a boy, he had lived through a famine and promised himself he would devote his life to feeding people. He knew that crossing two strains of rice would produce a hybrid and that hybrids enjoy something called "hybrid vigor," which allows them to give off much bigger crops. So all he had to do was cross two strains, take the seeds they produced, and get them to the farmers. But that would be extremely difficult, because the rice plant is self-pollinating. The sexual organs are so close together, he would have had to take pollen from one plant and apply it to another with tweezers. This was not a way to feed millions. He needed to find a rice plant that wouldn't pollinate itself.

His team searched the countryside, and an assistant came upon an unusual rice plant that had a sterile male organ. It could be pollinated by another plant from a different strain. Here's where the rope and beer bottle came in. He planted three kinds of rice in a pattern of alternating rows: When the plants were mature, two workers took opposite ends of a rope that had been weighted with a beer bottle and dragged it across the field, bending each row of rice toward the one behind it, pollinating it. Since the day he figured this out, his method has fed hundreds of millions of people across Asia.

I asked him if he knew of Jefferson. He smiled. "Yes. Jie Fu Sun," he said, calling him by his Chinese name. "Independence."

He was the only person I met in China who knew Jefferson. The real surprise, though, was learning that Yuan Long Ping had lived a life that in many ways paralleled Jefferson's.

As a young man studying to be a biologist, Yuan Long Ping was forced to learn Lysenkoism. This was the completely false theory of biology that said acquired changes could be passed on genetically to future generations. If you altered a plant, its offspring would have those same altered qualities. This idea probably appealed to leaders who bashed people over the head today to make good Communists out of future generations. So they decreed that Lysenko's nonscience was science.

"Lysenko. Now, I hate him," he told me. "Because he wasted my useful time—when I was young and strong."

But then, somehow, he found books on standard biology, and while he was working on Lysenkoism during the day, he taught himself true biology at night. "I bring **Lysenko's** book outside. But **inside** . . ."

This was a brave act; if he had been discovered, he could have been sent to prison, or worse. And I realized in that moment, standing ankle deep in an irrigation ditch in Jianjiang, that I was talking with a Chinese Jefferson. He had risked his life to give his countrymen rice that would save lives—and so had the man from Virginia.

Jefferson's side of the story began while he was in France. He was infatuated with Maria Cosway, a British artist, and in order to impress her while they were walking in the park, he tried to jump over a bush. This was not, you would think, the act of a genius. He caught his foot on the bush, fell, and broke his wrist. A short time later, he told people he was going to Italy to recuperate; but actually, he was on a secret mission. He had heard that Italy's Piedmont rice was better than the kind grown in the Carolinas, and he wanted some of that rice to plant in America. This was partly to help America compete with foreign countries in the sale of rice and partly because slavery, which he hated, was encouraged by the production of the American strain. The Carolina rice grew in hot, swampy, malarial lowlands, where slaves were becoming sick and dying. The Piedmont rice could be grown by ordinary farmers working without slaves in the highlands. He wanted that rice.

But the Italians were protective of their rice. It was forbidden, on pain of death, to leave Italy with unhusked rice in your possession. This was a tough sanction, and he ignored it. He sent two bags of it by mule to a port city, and just in case it was intercepted, he filled his pockets with as much as he could carry and brazenly crossed back into France.

Both men had taken serious risks, both over a question of improved rice and both to serve their country. Yuan seemed to have found the contentment that comes from serving others. I had to ask the typical interviewer's question: How does it feel to have helped so many people? He hesitated. In China, then, people weren't used to being asked about their feelings.

"You . . . you mean my feeling?"

"Yes. How do you feel?"

"My feeling. I feel very happy to do that. If people, they live very comfortable . . . this is my goal, my goal of my life, to make more people happy."

I told this story at Monticello, how I had finally understood Jefferson for the first time when I met this scientist standing in a muddy ditch on the other side of the world.

Just as Jefferson filled his pockets with forbidden rice, Yuan Long Ping filled his mind with forbidden ideas—placing himself in the same kind of danger.

Yuan has fed hundreds of millions of people . . . because he insisted on thinking for himself. He can say, as Jie Fu Sun once said, "I was bold in the pursuit of knowledge, never fearing to follow truth and reason to whatever results they led, and bearding every authority which stood in their way."

Meaning can happen when you least expect it. As with Julann's willingness to take a random walk, one improbable thing can lead to another. I found out a little about Jefferson when I started reading feverishly about him—but now I felt I could sense him, could feel his emotions. I could see his skin and hair; I could smell him. As great as he was, he was a man of complexities and contradictions; he was human. I could accept those contradictions more easily now because I'd found out how to imagine him in a more three-dimensional way.

And I got there in the oddest of ways. I scared myself.

Chapter 7

Where Is the Place of Understanding?

It's a quaint tradition that must go back centuries. You honor someone in a ceremony that includes seating him at a table on a dais, while the assembled guests watch him eat his dinner. That night they were honoring Simon Wiesenthal, and I was presenting him with an award, so the guests got to watch both of us eat. But, sitting next to him, I saw something more personal than that. I got to look into Wiesenthal's soul, and it changed me a little.

Thirty-seven years after Hitler brought his

country to ruin, a few neo-Nazis were still trying to kill one more Jew. They planted a bomb outside Wiesenthal's house in Vienna, so even in 1982, for him the war was not over. I had planned to speak about this, about how harshness and hatred persisted in this artful city of Mozart, Sacher torte, schnitzel, and strudel. But after my meal with Wiesenthal, I put aside what I had planned to say and spoke instead about the man who revealed himself to me in those few minutes. I had been asked once to play him in a movie on television, but I turned down the part because I didn't think I was right for it. As we talked now, I regretted that I hadn't said yes, just so I could have met him earlier.

Wiesenthal had escaped death in concentration camps and had spent his life tracking down Nazis who had never been brought to justice. His goal was not to ambush and kill them, but to deliver them to courts of law. He valued justice more than revenge. He might have **felt** like killing them, but he didn't. I had been advising young people for years to stick by their values. But **what** values? There are plenty of people in both prisons and palaces who follow their values, but not necessarily to anyone else's benefit. Here was a man whose life made it clear that it mattered what those values actually were; what they pointed you to. Just a few degrees in another direction and they could have led to a life of violent retribution. I wondered where this calibrated sense of values had come from.

As we talked, I saw a complicated person emerge. Wiesenthal's life was a serious, dangerous business, yet he was a man with a rich sense of humor. He told me he had a standing competition with an actor friend to see who could come up with the best jokes that the other had not heard before. Each time they met, they would pepper each other with new stories. And then he began telling me a long joke he had just come across. He loved the telling of it. Even the setup made his eyes crinkle with pleasure. He was about two-thirds of the way through the story when we noticed someone had come up to the dais and was waiting to speak to him. Wiesenthal turned to acknowledge him. The man was short and slight, in his seventies, with a weathered face. He smiled, but his smile was sorrowful.

"Remember me?" he asked.

Wiesenthal looked at him for a moment, and then tears welled in his eyes. "Yes."

They had known each other in one of the camps and had not met since then. They spoke only a few words. Considering the power it had over them, it was a surprisingly short exchange. The man said his name and a few words about the work he did now, and Wiesenthal nodded.

"I just wanted to say hello."

The man left and went to his table. Wiesenthal turned back to me. Tears were streaming down his face, but he didn't speak about the encounter with the man from the camp. Instead, he picked up where he had left off, and—through his tears—he finished telling the joke.

When I got up to speak, I told the audience what I had just seen. I thought it was a look not only into Wiesenthal's own person, but, in a way, into the soul of the whole Jewish people. No matter what the world had done to them, through their tears, they could find something to laugh at. There was almost no pain that couldn't be eased by humor. The ability to translate misery into something else gave them power over it.

When the evening was over and I was leaving the hall, a young rabbi came over to tell me he appreciated what I'd said. He told me a famous rabbi had a phrase that explained what made a good talk: "What comes from the heart goes to the heart."

That registered—and it stuck with me over the years. Maybe that was how Wiesenthal got his values—someone, at some time, revealing something from the heart that went to his.

I think that's how my daughters have found their values. As much as I tried, I don't think I put them there. Instead, I'll bet that everything they saw and heard resonated in the part of the brain that, because we don't know what else to call it, we call the heart. Wherever that particular **heart** is and whatever it is, I saw it develop in our girls from an early age.

I was having lunch with our daughter Beatrice when she was six. We were in a restaurant in California, and I was telling her about the wildlife that existed just outside our house. There was a column of flying insects that looked like gnats and clustered in a column, suspended in the air, right in the middle of the brick path leading to the street. They lived for a few weeks every summer, and then they were gone. Dead, I guess. And a year later there they were again, another column of them suspended in the same place. And there was a bird that built a nest every year over the lamp by the front door. She fluttered up and flew out past your ear when you left the house. Her nest was woven tightly. It was made of twigs, and she had no hands to weave it with, only claws and a beak. How did she do it? Once, when it fell out of the cranny between the lamp and the wall, all the eggs broke apart, but not the nest.

I was carried away by the wonder of it, but suddenly I realized that tears were coming down Bea's face. I'd been talking about nature, but I'd included death in the story. The dead gnats, the chicks in their broken eggs. Had that upset her? She tried, but she couldn't tell me why she was crying. Maybe at that time in her world, death wasn't part of the wonder of nature. It didn't seem fair to her.

Even as a child, Bea had a sense of fairness. We taught her to argue for what she wanted, and she took to arguing like a lawyer. As young as seven or eight, she argued her case meticulously and felt that since her arguments were unassailable, she should get what she was asking for. Anything else would be unfair. And fairness still guides her in her work. She led a group of women in building a children's museum and spent ten years fighting the opposition of interests with connections all the way up to the governor. They won, and the museum serves thousands of children a year now.

I wanted to pass on values to Bea's kids. And my first inclination was to do it the way I did with Bea: by talking. As soon as they were old enough to reason, I would take them after school to a local muffin shop and we'd have tea and talk about ethical issues. This sounds monumentally boring, but they seemed to be interested. A favorite of theirs was the lady who sued a fast-food chain because one of their restaurants sold her a cup of scalding hot coffee that burned her seriously. Was she in the right? Or was the restaurant? In each round of discussions, we would worry about new information that made the issue more complicated, until it was almost impossible to know what was fair. All I wanted, of course, was for them to think about fairness, but I doubt they'll get it from talking. They'll get it indirectly, by what they see happen spontaneously around them, because what comes from the heart goes to the heart.

Bea's house is full of noise and life. A fire is going in the kitchen. The kids are laughing, fighting, bargaining, complaining. And meanwhile, as the household swirls around him, Bosco is watching it all with one blue eye and one brown eye. He doesn't know from fairness. He just wants to lick your face. He's a mutt, a cross between a dog that looks like a frankfurter and one that looks like a hamburger. But he's all affection. He runs across the room toward you, pees on the floor with excitement, and rolls over on his back so you can scratch his belly. He's been trained by a professional dog guru, and when someone in the family looks him in his mismatched eyes and says in an unmistakable tone, "Place!" he skitters back to his place, which is a small piece of carpet in the corner. He stays there obediently, straining against an invisible leash that exists only in his trained brain, as he longs to curl in the crook of your arm. To him, I guess, fairness is whatever comes his way. But it seems hard to let him languish there.

How long he stays in his place depends on how long the children can go without giving him a thought. They may not feel like dropping what they're doing to give him the attention he craves. He depends on their ability to know, like Wiesenthal, the difference between what they feel like doing and what they know is fair. I watch and wait for them to notice his suffering and take him in their arms.

They don't let him wait too long. They're learning to feel for a fellow animal. And seeing them learn that, just as I watched Bea learn it, adds just a bit of feeling to my own life that it's been worth living it.

Chapter 8

"Love Your Art, Poor as It May Be"

Sometimes, standing on the stage, I have an experience of unusual awareness. I know I'm in a theater and that an audience is watching; and I know that the woman across from me is not really who she's claiming to be. And in spite of knowing we're in front of other people, I know we're alone in this room. I'm also aware of something much weirder than that. I'm aware that the two of us are other people, someplace else, arguing over something. We are so completely involved with this struggle, we could say almost anything at this moment. But we say the same thing we said last night. And I'm aware that this is because we're acting. It's like an endless arc of images in paired mirrors curving off into infinity. And when this moment is at its most intense, it's at its lightest. There is no strain; in fact, there's a feeling of floating. But, of course, I'm aware that, far from floating, I'm standing on a stage that's raked for the audience to see us better, and I have to be careful where I plant my feet or I'll lose my balance.

This multiple awareness is for me the ecstasy of acting. When this happens, there doesn't seem to be any part of my brain that isn't working on something. The clock stops, and an intricate pas de deux takes place in slow motion. You choke with emotion, yet you feel nothing. You know everything and nothing at once. You walk a narrow beam a hundred stories high, but your steps are as sure as on a sidewalk. Failure can't happen. Death is remote. There is no way to know what you'll say next; and then you say it. And you notice that you're saying it slightly differently from the last time you said it at exactly this moment.

This is what it was like for me the year I played in **Art** at the Royale Theatre on Broadway. Each night, I was dropped off at the entrance to the alleyway and walked down the narrow space between a neighboring theater and a bar, past huge bins sometimes overflowing with the rancid trash from the matinees of three theaters. Inside the stage door, I would write my name on the sign-in sheet, say hello to the doorman, and head up the stairs to my dressing room. Then, within a few minutes, Victor Garber, Alfred Molina, and I would be sitting on straight-backed chairs in a tiny room, where we would lock in a session of ribald laughter and merciless rudeness that would last for an hour. We never talked about the play; we just made fun of one another. And then a few minutes before the curtain went up, we would throw on our stage clothes and resume the jousting until a second before the curtain went up on my first lines to the audience. As Victor and Fred came onstage, it was as though we had never dropped the connection we had backstage. We were alive to one another, flushed with the present moment. We took hands like skydivers—and went up instead of down.

Once you taste this beautiful madness, you want it again and again. It's delicious. And in that moment when nothing else exists but you and them, and yet everything exists, that's a moment when you know what it is to be alive.

Whenever they ask me to talk to young people who are learning about the theater, I go, hoping to find the words that explain what makes this happen to me. I'm hoping, of course, that it might happen to them, too.

I don't try to teach them acting. I'm not so sure I **can** teach. Once, when I was doing a play in London, the Royal Academy of Dramatic Art asked me to come and talk to their kids. The night before, I went to sleep thinking of what I'd say. As usual, I wanted to tell them something they'd remember forever. And when I sat down in front of them, I said, "I'm going to tell you something you'll never forget. It's an acronym: A. C. T." And then for an hour I spelled out what each of those letters meant. The only problem is that I haven't any idea now what I told them. As a memory aid, it seems to have been a disaster. "A" might have stood for dramatic action, and I think "C" was concentration, but what could "T" have been? "Try Not to Forget Your Lines"? I don't think I'm a teacher.

But I do like to infect people with enthusiasm. I'm avid about being avid.

So in 1998, during the run of **Art**, when Victor and Fred and I were having this extraordinary experience of utter and total connection, and the

American Academy of Dramatic Arts asked me to talk to their graduating class, I went.

The academy had a special place in my heart, but not because I ever went there.

> **Forty years ago when I was starting out as an actor, I wanted to enroll at the American Academy of Dramatic Arts as a student, but I couldn't afford the tuition. I couldn't really afford the bus fare to get down there. I also had the misguided idea that if I trained as an actor, the training would somehow rob me of my natural genius. So as a result, I was self-taught, and it took an extra ten or twenty years to get rid of some of the bad habits and pretentious mannerisms I had, many of which came from my natural genius.**

I didn't want to swamp them all at once with talk of ecstasy, so I noodled for a while on the edges.

> **I think I would offer just one or two little suggestions. One has to do with energy. Laurence Olivier said that the actor's job is**

to supply the audience with energy—and some people think he might have been overly generous in that area, sometimes giving us more than our money's worth. But energy is a fact of nature. Nothing takes place without energy. On the stage, just as in the rest of nature, there's no chemistry without energy. But, as in science, it has to be appropriate and sufficient. It has to be genuine, truthful. The energy some actors avoid is the fake, actorish energy of a century ago. But it's not necessary for us to mute our energy. Muted energy comes off as a form of stage fright, and it often is. Instead of muting it, we need to tune it to the right frequency.

We ought to avoid underacting with the same determination with which we avoid overacting. It's just as boring. In fact, the greatest pleasure onstage comes from being able to drop acting altogether and just zero in on the other person and on what you want from them and, given everything your character is capable of, get it in the best way you can.

Then I got a little closer to the real thrill of the thing.

People have been analyzing acting for at least a couple of centuries now and sometimes arguing about the best way to do it. The debate is often divided between a view of acting as an internal process and an external one. But I don't know if the good actors I've worked with are that much different from one another. One way or another, we all seem to get transformed by our imaginations. When we're cooking, something happens deep in our brains that affects us profoundly. Sometimes it happens as a result of studying the psychology of the character, and sometimes it's just putting on the clothes. Suddenly, there's a glorious moment where acting falls away and you're speaking with utter simplicity. Fancy acting can often feel seductively grand (for the actor and even sometimes for the audience). But for me, simplicity is the greatest joy for us all.

Everybody knows that. Or at least we've heard it often enough: Simplicity is everything. But how do we get there?

Jimmy Cagney used to say, "Just stand there and tell the truth," which for most of us is easier said than done. But is acting telling the truth or just lying well? Some actors I've met are convinced that being a good liar is the same as being a good actor. I don't think so, but maybe acting is like the rest of life: The rewards go to those who can tell the truth and also tell an occasional lie when absolutely necessary. Either way, it's still not easy to tell the truth.

Sometimes we're too anxious to even know what the truth is. Anxiety is a powerful toxin. You can think you're calm, in command of the moment, and be undergoing an anxiety attack as big as the Norman conquest. Learn what makes you anxious, learn how to control it, or it will control you. You've probably already developed defenses against anxiety that seem useful to you. They may even seem attractive—little smiles and perky gestures—but you'll feel better when you can drop them. There's no power like the power of the calm and confident. Jack Nicholson said acting is 90 percent nerve. Sometimes when I'm anxious, I remember that and it helps. It helps, as I go to sleep sometimes, simply to say to myself, I can do it. I've done it before, and I can do it now.

Love getting better at it, not getting praised for it. I learned that from my father, who began his career in burlesque. The comics would say of a performer who was constantly looking for praise that he was always taking bows. I learned from my father that if you're just looking to take bows, you'll almost always be disappointed, because the applause is never loud enough. The bow is really just a gracious ritual. If it becomes your goal, it's a drug. The performance itself offers an ecstasy far greater than the drug of the bow after the performance is done. Look instead to love the connection you can have with the other actor, with the moment itself.

That moment can happen when you perform an art. Any art. It's a moment like no other.

And the better you get at it, the better it feels. But to say you can perform an art isn't as grand as it sounds. It's just a good connection between your brain and your fingertips that lets you do something that lifts the spirit. Like pitching a really beautiful fastball. I've come to believe that it doesn't matter how simple the art is, it's worth all the affection I can lavish on it.

When I was young, Actors' Equity had a quote on the cover of their magazine. Always the same one. Each month, when the magazine came in the mail, I studied the cover for a few minutes and thought about it. It said, "Love your art, poor as it may be." I may have the words wrong, and I forget who originally said it—it was either a Roman or Shakespeare talking like a Roman. But loving your art, no matter how humble it is, can transform you. It's worth the trouble it takes. It's true it can sometimes bring you despair, but it can also bring you ecstasy, just the way loving a person can.

I knew if I kept talking about ecstasy like this, I was going to make them think they could get there in some abstract way. I wanted them to understand that you have to take simple, concrete steps. For humans, flying isn't magic; it's physics.

It helps to remember a few basic things about acting. Show up on time. Know your lines. Respect your fellow actor, your director, and yourself.

Please, do respect your fellow actors. We're part of a vast, convivial community. We've all run the same gauntlet, and we've all had to contend with the unemployment office, unhelpful employers, critics, landlords, and tax collectors. When your friends are up for a part, encourage them. When you're in a play, give the other actors the stage when it's theirs; when it's your turn, take the stage with gusto—and then give it back to them. And when you go backstage after a show to see actors, you've got to remember you're entering a burn ward. These people are raw, and this is not the time to analyze their work. You hug them and say, "You were wonderful." You have to say You, you have to say were, and you have to say wonderful.

Don't try to be honest. The actor is a

raw, open wound after a performance. You can't say, "The play was wonderful." That means you're deliberately avoiding talking about the actor. You can't say, "You are wonderful." That means he's wonderful in general, but not tonight. And you have to say wonderful (brilliant is okay, too, but nothing less). No one needs to hear they were interesting or that they looked as though they were having a good time.

You probably even need to say, "The play was wonderful," even if it was a turkey. Never forget that when you go back after a play, you're talking to the walking wounded.

And when you're acting, remember that it's play. Enjoy it, and enjoy it deeply, richly. Use your intellect as well as your emotions. Try to find out what connects the Apollonian and the Dionysian; the serious and the antic. One without the other is not as satisfying. There are at least a couple of ways of looking at the actor. One is as a priest performing rituals of reconciliation, enlightenment, and dedication . . . or as a clown performing acts of rudeness, appetite, and functions of the body. Find ways of serving as both.

There's an ecstasy to acting, and that ecstasy is a glorious experience, but acting is something else, too. It's a service to the people who come to the theater. Acting may look like the parade of the vanities, but in fact it can be a noble calling. To be able to be another person on the stage, to let an audience feel that person's vulnerability, that person's follies, that person's courage, fear, strength, lunacy, as their own is to give them a chance to understand better what it means to be human.

It had taken me a long time to understand what I was telling them that day. My education in the theater started when I was nine, stepping onto the stage with my father and feeling the warmth from both the spotlight and the audience. We were entertaining soldiers and sailors during the war. Performing next to him, I felt my father's love. He was expressing it through sharing the stage with me and allowing me into his profession. This was, I think, the most intimate he could get. He seemed embarrassed to express emotion or love in other ways.

As I got older, I was carried along by the pleasure of my contact with the audience. My sense of worth was reinforced by knowing I could please them, so I became good at making them laugh. I knew instantly how pleased they were. But it was still mostly about me.

When I got older, there was a turning point—a realization that when I went onstage, it wasn't entirely for me: I had a service to perform. I still got pleasure out of it. It was still intoxicating, but now I began to realize I was also there for these other people, out in the dark of the audience. I'm not sure when this thought first came to me, but I think it was in my twenties when I saw the film **Pather Panchali** by the Indian director Satyajit Ray. There was a moment toward the end of the story when the father returns from a long trip away from home with gifts for his daughter, who he finds out has died in his absence. The simple power of his realization that he has missed his daughter's illness and death hit me hard. I knew instantly that it was possible to be absent without ever leaving home. In my own way, I might have been as cool with my children as my father had been with me. A feeling of rawness stayed with me for days. It was as if something in me that I didn't need had been ripped out of me. A way of behaving that wasn't good for me or those I loved had been removed, not gently by persuasion, but in an instant, with violence. For a few days, at least, I had been changed by the experience of simply watching a movie. If I could go through this, sitting in the audience, what must other people be going through? It was somewhere around this time that I began to understand that the audience wasn't only there for me; I could be there for them.

I had to find a way to put this into words decades later. In 2006, I was invited to another academy. I was asked to join the American Academy of Arts and Sciences. Each year, in a tradition that goes back to John Adams, a new group of artists, scholars, and scientists is brought in, and I was asked to speak at the induction ceremony representing all of us from the arts and humanities. This scared me. I wrote about a dozen drafts, each one lamer than the other. Then I remembered what I had learned about my own art, poor as it was: that I was there to perform a service. And when I thought about that, I realized how much alike the humanist scholars and the artists really are. We're all trying to answer similar questions, and we probably had very similar origins.

It wasn't long ago, not even a tick of the cosmic clock, after we first appeared on

this wet rock spinning through space and time, that one of us put his handprint on the wall of a cave. Whatever else it meant, that handprint said, "I'm here." But even before that, there must have been dance and song. There must have been vocalization; the hubbub of community; the glee of existence. All this, I think, was the birth of the arts.

We made notches on sticks to count and keep track of things, but the notches we made in our brains were the crucial ones. We began parsing our language so that, in a string of sounds, the order of those sounds had meaning. This let us communicate the huge difference between "My foot is on the rock" and "The rock is on my foot." At that point, I would think, we could start parsing not just our words, but the world itself. We could go from the statement of "I'm here" to questions like "Where is here, what is here?"—"What's that over there?"—and the big one: "Who am I who is asking all these questions?" And that, I think, was the birth of the humanities.

We have all traveled different paths in search of an answer to a question that has nagged us for thousands of years: What does it mean to be human? Together with our colleagues in the sciences, we search endlessly for an answer to that question: What does it mean to be human? It may be the most critical question we've ever asked in the life of our species, especially now— when our ability to destroy ourselves is so much greater than our ability to understand ourselves.

Here's what gets me about artists: I'm touched by the artist's courage and generosity.

This is what it's like when you decide to be an artist: First of all, you don't decide to do it. You're kidnapped by it. You never know if you have what it takes. After years of doing it, you're always back where you started, a beginner. Because every time you head for the horizon, it's not there.

An artist looks at life and the chaos of nature, then takes a brush, a violin, a camera, or his or her own body and plays a plaintive song of desire on it. A desire for understanding. Who are we? Why are we the way we are? Can we ever become what we wish we could be?

All artists, I think, are poets—whether they arrange words on a page, make steel and stone into buildings, or leap into the air, transforming their bodies into visual music.

The poet puts the right words in the right order so that the colliding of their sounds and meaning makes your neurons flash like a pinball machine. And like the poet, artists of all kinds take the viewer's nervous system and snap it like a whip. They refresh our vision. They press our reset button. They make the colors of the world as vivid as they were when we were children and saw them for the first time.

Artists try to say things that can't be said. In a fragile net of words, gestures, or colors, we hope to capture a feeling; a taste; a painful longing. But the net is always too porous, and we're left with the sweet frustration of almost knowing, which is teasingly pleasurable.

We often tune ourselves to the oscillations of nature: the rhythmic beat of the heart—or the sea running up the shore, then pulling back—or the bang and slam of the shutter in a storm. From these elemental rhythms spring the one-two beat of music and the push and pull of a play on words. They're the antagonist and protagonist of drama. They're the essay's ebb and flow of argument.

We ride this rhythm—and it rides us. Like a wind sock in a heartless gale, the artist whips back and forth to the beat of nature, free of care and, sometimes, just as free of safety. I love my fellow artists for the dangerous life they lead; for the exhaustion of their birth pains; and for how they bet their lives on the slim hope they can make something worth looking at or listening to.

We may amuse and delight, but, like Shakespeare's clowns, we also ask the most impertinent questions about who we think we are. Where would we be without artists? We would be gray automatons in a gray landscape picking gray flowers for gray lovers. Life would be grim.

And where would we be without the humanities? Life, I think, would seem far more meaningless. The search for wisdom—and for a deeper understanding of who we are—is the daunting challenge for the humanities. They are that part of our

141

common brain that reflects on our actions, questions our desires, and forces us to declare what we value. In some ways, we're all artists—practicing our skills, but also reaching into the dark for an answer.

In the dark of the cave, we hope to find light—not from the torch, but from the sparks that fly as we decode the handprint on the wall.

I wish us luck.

So I guess I felt that day in a rush of optimism that art can, at least, make life less meaningless. And maybe it can. But I have to be honest with myself. It isn't all the high-flown talk about humanity that makes me feel alive. It's really just the moment of play, when everything else disappears for a while. That's when a lightness overtakes me and I'm standing beside myself, watching. I see myself commit little mistakes, but I don't judge them. And I see little moments that are surprisingly good. But I don't judge them, either. I just notice them. Everything happening is good because it leads to something else. And so it comes back again and again to the ecstasy of it.

But I wonder if even that's enough.

At eleven o'clock the curtain is down, and

you're walking back down the ugly little alley from the stage door to the street. You're in the world again. If you've been very lucky, you've had a couple of hours where time stood still for you. But now it's over. And it's not true that life is short but art is long. Powers fail, and passion gets spent. Life is short, and art is even shorter.

Isn't there anything that will get us through to the very end? I kept looking.

Chapter 9

The Meaning of Life in a Glass of Water

They were buildings so tall, they had thrown out television signals across all of New York City and beyond, so simple and staunch that one glimpse of them, in a movie or on a souvenir plate, instantly said, **This is New York.** One by one, they descended to the ground, billowing an ugly, toxic cloud while disbelief and confusion rose in each of us from a place in our chest where once we had felt safety and comfort.

The towers came down, carrying with them the lives of people who had left us not at the end of their time, or even in an unexpected accident, but in an act of ignorant, malicious hatred. When that happened, a little patch of meaning seemed to come loose from us, like a layer of skin gone dead. Remember how after the disbelief came a desperate urge to **do** something? We all felt it. It was intolerable to think there was no action you could take. Out in the countryside where we lived, I went with three of my granddaughters to a shoe store. The girls were four, seven, and nine years old, and we gravely picked out a dozen pairs of heavy work boots for the rescue workers. We brought them to a truck parked across from the village commons, where two women on the back of the truck were hoisting up contributions meant for Ground Zero. In the days that followed the attack, so many people sent truckloads of boots, blankets, and work clothes that trucks piled up along the Hudson and many tons of supplies never made it across the river from a warehouse in New Jersey. But it hadn't been wasted effort, because we all needed to take some kind of action. The satirical website The Onion published a fake news article that, while it may have been meant to be funny, captured with poignancy our desperation. It told of a woman in Topeka, Kansas, who felt so helpless, so in need of doing something, that she baked a cake. Then she covered it with strawberries and food coloring in the shape of an American flag. Like her, and like millions of others, I made American flags, too. I went to a website and printed out flags that I taped to the rear windows of the family cars. I nailed a pole to the fence at the end of our driveway and tied a hardware-store flag to it.

As you walked the city in the days following the attack, you would see dozens of flags thirty stories high in the windows of apartment buildings. People had pasted the flags to their windows on the chance that someone would look up and know that someone else was pulling for them. During these weeks, the flag had stopped being an expression of particular political leanings; it belonged to all of us again.

Three weeks after the attack, I got a phone call from the actor Richard Masur. He had been on the site since the rescue work began and had been volunteering to organize help for the rescue workers. He asked if I wanted to come down and talk with the workers on the site and show support. I did; and a couple of nights later, I was on a boat with a small group of theater people. As we made our way down the Hudson to what had become known as "the pile," I didn't know what to expect. We were going there mainly to listen, to give people a chance to talk and unburden themselves.

The boat docked, and we walked for a few blocks among darkened downtown buildings. Then we turned a corner, and the sight hit us. Work lights illuminated the scene almost as if it were day. Steel shards reached many stories high, piercing the black sky. Climbing over the wreckage were firefighters, police, and construction workers from all over the country; cranes were lifting huge pieces of debris. They were removing the concrete and steel carefully, because under it were the remains of colleagues, sons, daughters, brothers, and sisters.

I went into a tent where workers were taking a break and sat down with a cup of tea across from a young police officer. He had lost his partner when the buildings fell. I offered him the chance to talk about it, hoping it would give him some relief, but I immediately regretted it. His face was flushed, his eyes were strained, and he spoke almost as if it were his duty to recount the details of his loss to anyone who asked. I saw no relief in his face, only pain. I spent a few more minutes with him, thanked him for what he was doing for all of us, and excused myself. I didn't want to prolong his sadness. He needed a professional to listen to him, not a well-meaning amateur.

I went out to the edge of the pile and shook hands with a few of the workers. Someone handed me a phone and asked me to say hello to his wife. I could hear in her voice that she missed her husband and worried about him. After the call, I asked if they were getting all the supplies they needed. They said they were doing all right, but one of the men mentioned how much they'd enjoyed a few candy bars someone had sent over. The others agreed and said they were sorry they'd run out. I was surprised at how such a small thing had given them a lift.

After a few minutes, I excused myself and stepped away because, again, I had the impression they were accommodating me by talking with me, and I had come somehow to accommodate them. I was off by myself when a man in his fifties came over, put out his hand, and introduced himself. His name was Johnnie Bell, an ironworker. His face was lined with days of nonstop work on the site, and he spoke softly.

"Can I ask you something? Look at that—" He pointed over to the pile. "There are people here from all over the country. They figured they were needed here, and they came. Some of them haven't seen their families in weeks." His eyes locked on mine. "It would be awful if we lost this spirit of pulling together after all this gets cleaned up. We're one country now." I thought of the flags we had all put out. We were one community again, one nation. "It doesn't matter now about religion or race or things like that," Johnnie said. "We gotta **stay** this way. I don't hear anybody saying that."

I promised him that when I got the chance to say in public what he'd just told me, I would do it. Then I got back on the boat and went uptown, still wishing there were something more concrete I could do.

The next day, I made phone calls until I tracked down someone at the Hershey factory in Pennsylvania. I told her how much a few candy bars had meant to the workers and asked if her company could send a truckload of Hershey bars to the site. She said they'd wanted to but that they had sent only hard candy because of the pileup of trucks. They were afraid that in the sun's heat, the chocolate bars would melt. I gave her the address of a warehouse forty blocks north where we had embarked for Ground Zero the night before. The shipment could be kept cool there. She thanked me, and a truckload of Hershey bars was dispatched to the workers. I had accomplished my own version of baking a cake.

A sense of helplessness can be overwhelming in an emergency, and we take action, sometimes any action, to hold off that feeling. A need to act seems built into us. Just getting from birth to death can seem like one grand emergency, and action is how many of us make our way.

Will Durant published a book in 1932 called **On the Meaning of Life,** in which intellectuals and artists of the time told him what meaning life had for each of them. One of the simplest and most honest statements was a letter to Durant from Carl Laemmle, the movie mogul. In it, he said he was happy to do business and make money, but most of all, simply to work. Work gave him all the meaning he needed. And he preferred that to "the sourness and hopelessness that comes with too much abstract thinking."

A life of action may not seem synonymous with meaning, although a lot of us act as if it were. And for all I know, it is. It seems right that Laemmle would focus on action—because he was a moviemaker. Twenty-four hundred years ago, the Greek dramatists saw the importance of action in our lives and mined it. In the theater they created, they invented a ritual of action that to this day captures our attention like nothing else, with maybe the exception of sports, the other great ritual of action formalized by the Greeks.

A couple of years after 9/11, I was asked to speak to writers at Southampton College. And I asked if I could talk about the essential ingredient of drama: action.

Dramatic action is not, of course, found in scenes of running, jumping, and crashing. Dramatic action takes place more in the mind than in the muscles. And it's as essential to good dramatic writing as are great ideas and grand themes; even more so. After roaming the stage for fifty years, trying to keep audiences alive, I've learned that if the play is not rooted in dramatic action, no one will watch it.

Standing in the wings from the time I was a child, I saw actors holding the audience's attention. They did it almost effortlessly, and at first I couldn't tell what the essential ingredient was. Then, when I was eighteen and my eyes were opened to the world of ideas, I read Aristotle's **Poetics,** and I felt as though a secret code had been whispered into my ear by a man who'd been dead for 2,400 years.

I wanted to tell all this to the writers at Southampton College, but it seemed dry and intellectualized. As we drove to the college, I told Arlene I didn't know how to make it vivid to them. She was driving the car, and as usual, she had an unerring sense of direction. "Why don't you think of an image you can start with?" I thought about that, and by the time we got to the college, her question had led to one of the best moments in any of these talks I've given, because it was a moment in which I said nothing.

I came out onstage and asked for a volunteer, someone relatively brave. A young man came up from the front row, and I poured him a glass of water from a pitcher. I asked him to walk with the glass to the other side of the stage. He was a little self-conscious, and there were a few titters from the audience.

Then I crossed over to him and filled his glass to the very brim. There wasn't a millimeter of space between the water and the rim of the glass. "Okay," I told him, "now walk to that table over there and put the glass down—but don't spill a drop."

The table was all the way on the other side of the stage. The water was so high in the glass that it didn't seem possible to take even a step without spilling it. I upped the imaginary ante: "If you spill anything, your entire village will die." He and the audience chuckled at this attempt at melodrama, but having been given a challenge, he really didn't want to spill the water. Slowly he moved forward, and there was utter silence in the auditorium. Thirty yards away, six hundred people were focused on the rim of the glass tumbler. When his hand tilted slightly and a small bead of water started slowly down the side of the glass, you could hear a gasp from the crowd. Agonizingly slowly, but with mounting tension in the house, he made it to the table and put down the glass of water. There was thunderous applause.

I asked the audience to decide which trip across the stage had been more involving, more interesting. For me, the difference between these two identical physical actions was in the desire, the wholehearted striving, to achieve something. Dramatic action started in his brain and radiated to his toes and his fingertips. It made his every motion something we couldn't take our eyes off.

For years, as an actor, I'd had to find ways to take lines that had no action in them and find the action. Now, speaking to fellow writers, I was imploring them to look for the action before handing off the play to the cast. What is this character after? How is he trying to get it? Without that knowledge somewhere in your bones,

153

the play runs out of gas and chokes to a stop. The hardest are plays in which the playwright feels it's necessary to tell the audience things the characters already know. It seems almost impossible to write a historical drama without saying things like "Well, Mr. Lincoln, the war has been on for three weeks now." What is Lincoln supposed to reply to that? "You're kidding. Three weeks? I haven't been getting the paper lately."

Bald-faced exposition, where the author brings us up-to-date by making the actors fire off a barrage of information that they would never bother to mention if an audience weren't listening, is often considered allowable—sometimes even a necessary part of constructing a story. But I asked the writers in the hall at Southampton that night to think radically and actually forbid themselves exposition. David Mamet says that plays should start late and finish early. And by that I think he means: Get in **after** the exposition and leave **before** the neat wrapping up. I think so, too. At the very least, I told them, let the opening scene of **Othello** be your guide. Roderigo and Iago are fighting about money. Roderigo is tired of paying him to plead his case with Othello. And in the course of their fight, in order to prove his point and keep the money, Iago makes it clear how tough a person Othello is to work on and manipulate, and we know everything we need to know about Othello and Iago, but it's all been active.

I think before any actor enters into a scene, it should be necessary to pass under a sign in the wings that reads, "You are not allowed on this stage unless you want something with all your heart and soul—and have a way of getting it." Right before I go onstage, I almost always ask myself, **What am I going out there to do? How am I going to get what I want?** Even in a mostly one-man play like **QED,** where I played the physicist Richard Feynman and talked to the audience for two hours, I asked myself what I wanted from them—the real people I'd be talking to. I think this question is what makes a play move forward. More than that, dramatic action even tells you who the character is, because what people want and how they go about getting it is a way of saying who they are. (And like so much of what I've learned onstage, this is true of life as well.)

All this has to be felt personally, though, not clinically. I always know I'm close to being able to play a character not when I merely feel that I could want what he wants, but that I **do** want it and, in fact, that I **deserve to have it.** Then, depending on the kind of play you're in, either you get it or you don't. The difference between comedy and tragedy is that in a comedy, people usually get what they want; in a tragedy, they get what they deserve.

One night, I stood in someone's elegant beach house in Water Mill, New York, and glared at Annabella Sciorra. It didn't matter that I really cared for her; she hadn't returned my love, and I had been so wounded by her, I deserved to make her pay for it. A wave of righteous anger rose in me that made me want to destroy the room we were in, which I did, and then I chased her down the beach with a pickax. We were acting a scene in a movie while all this was going on. We would chat and joke between shots, but somewhere in my brain, through an act of imagination, what I wanted was real to me. I didn't have to brood about how I **felt**—I was doing. The doing didn't flow from feeling, the feeling came from doing.

As we were about to do the shot where I chased her across the sand, Annabella, who was twenty-eight years younger than me, warned me she was going to run fast and that I probably wouldn't be able to catch her. I said, "You'd better run as fast as you can. I'm going to catch you." After all, I deserved to catch her. And I did—way before she reached the spot where the camera was waiting for us. We had to do it again, and this time she ran for her life. I caught her again and tackled her (bruising my rib and getting a load of sand in my eye, which limits somewhat the physical prowess part of the story), and then I tried to kill her with the pickax. But her character was destined by the script to get what she wanted and mine to get what he deserved. I wound up floating in the ocean with the ax embedded in my skull. Planting the fake rubber ax on my head was a three-hour job in the makeup chair. But before we finished shooting the scene, we had to break for lunch, which on a night shoot like this can occur at two in the morning. It would take too long to take off the ax and then spend three hours putting it back, so it was assumed by everyone that I would have lunch without removing it. Not only lunchtime, but all of reality is altered on a movie set. I stood calmly at the window of the food truck, holding out my tray, with the ax sticking out of my head, and asked, "Do you have vegetables to go with that?"

I wonder if the Greeks who evolved this action-based form of storytelling also saw it as the way we live the stories of our lives, outside the theater. We seem made for action. All living things seem made for it. Every amoeba and every little nematode is looking for something, whether it's plodding and slithering toward food for the here and now or the survival of its genes for eternity. I can't believe that every person alive isn't striving for something. I wouldn't be surprised to learn that somewhere inside a catatonic is a person putting a great deal of energy into avoiding pain.

When actors behave in a lifelike way, they do it through action, and a few weeks after September eleventh, when a time came for actors to respond to the worst act of war on our shores, they did it through the only action they knew.

On a clear, cold morning in October, the casts of Broadway shows gathered to shoot a television spot. The mayor had said that New York City was back in business. Not just the theater, but all the hotels and the restaurants, too. Cabdrivers, travel agents, shopkeepers . . . all the trades that are in sync with, that rise and fall with, the rhythms and tunes of Broadway . . . they were all back. And to get out the word, five hundred Broadway performers were being asked to shoot a television spot in Duffy Square in Manhattan, with all the glitz of Times Square behind us, belting out Kander and Ebb's "New York, New York."

As I headed to the Booth Theatre, where we were to meet, I wasn't sure I wanted to put on a face that hid the sadness we all were carrying around. I didn't feel much like singing. But as the Booth filled with actors, singers, and dancers, we all began to realize we were at an event unlike any we'd ever experienced before.

In one corner of the theater were the Rockettes, in other parts of the theater the casts of **Beauty and the Beast, The Rocky Horror Show, The Producers . . .** people from show after show were there, many of them in costume. Some had worked together the night before, and some had never met. Some of us hadn't seen one another in years, since we had started out making the rounds together on foot, looking for our first jobs. People were climbing over seats, hugging, consoling, and kidding one another.

The choreographer came onstage and ran through a couple of dance steps he wanted us to do. A great laugh and cheer went up for the sheer Broadwayness of it. I panicked. I was still trying to learn the words of the song. Now I had to remember dance steps?

One by one, our shows were called out of the theater. We walked past alleyways where we had once stood in line to audition in days past. Finally we arrived, feeling like kids again, at Duffy Square, where dance captains would go over the routine that five hundred of us were expected to perform in unison a few minutes later.

With relief, I noticed that even a couple of experienced dancers were having trouble remembering when our hands were supposed to shoot out. "Is it **Up, hands; Down, hands** . . . New York, or is it **Up, hands,** New . . . **Down, hands,** York?"

A couple of nine-year-olds from **Les Mis** had the routine down within minutes. I asked them to coach me.

People were mixing, trading jokes, comparing costumes. Like characters who had stepped out of their stories, an actor from **The Lion King** and one from **Beauty and the Beast** were touching each other's faces, each examining the other's elaborate, heavy mask. While they talked, a child actor helpfully held the Beast's tail for him.

In the chill morning air, dancers, male and female, with hardly any clothing to cover them, were practicing their moves and doing bits for one another. For the first time in what seemed like a long time, we were able to be antic again.

Every few minutes, a cheer went up and the actors applauded and waved their arms. A fire truck was going by, carrying heroes on their way downtown.

During a break, a couple of firefighters from

Buffalo came over and asked to have their picture taken with us. Had they been working down-town? I asked. Yes. After a twelve-hour day in Buf-falo, they'd had a bus ride to New York and fifteen straight hours on the pile. They hadn't slept in at least two days. The pockets of flesh under their eyes were purple with fatigue. They were modest and shy. We embraced them, wanting them to know how proud they made us, probably wanting some of their strength to rub off on us.

Finally, we were ready to do a take. We had prerecorded the song, but we sang our hearts out anyway, cursing under our breath if our arms went up when they should have gone down.

As we sang, the choreographer coached us with terms I'd never heard before. "Sunshine and rain!" he called out. "Sunshine and rain!" (You rock for-ward as your hands go up to the sun and then you rock back as your hands go behind you and down toward the ground. Sunshine and rain.)

We got to the end of the song. "Come on . . . come . . . through . . . New York, New York!" We raised our arms on the last, long-held note, but he called out to us, "Not so **fast**! Slowly. Make 'em **beg** for it!" We collapsed in laughter. For a few healing hours, we'd been allowed into the sacred order of Broadway gypsies.

We did our final take, said good-bye, and broke up—more slowly than we might have on a normal shoot. On the way home, I thought about how much the day had given me. All we had done was show up, sing, and move a little. The real work, the heartbreaking work, was going on a couple of miles south of us. I knew that what we had done was trivial. But on the other hand, this is what we **do,** and doing it with all the energy we could give it had lifted us up. We had been in motion; we had taken action— and here and there, color began to come back to this wounded, gray city.

For a while, at least, life was a little less meaningless.

Chapter 10

When the Breeze Was Scarce, I Named the Boat Patience

The first time I met him, he was sitting behind a lacquered desk shaped like a large kidney. It wasn't so much a desk as a shiny beige fortress of power and glitz. I was inside my own fortress of youthful self-confidence that only an out-of-work actor with no prospects could possess.

We both knew nothing much could come of this meeting. Arlene's mother had asked me to see him. She and her husband, Simon, were friends with the Bregmans, a couple who lived in their building in the Bronx. They traveled together and played cards every week. The couple's son had done well in the insurance business, but he had always been interested in show business and wanted to be a manager. Apparently, he had helped a few actors and singers get work. Arlene's mother urged me to see him at his office. "He can help you," she said. "Please see him. Martin Bregman. He knows people."

So here I was at his insurance office. And there he was behind the beige kidney. We both smiled at the confidence his mother and Arlene's mother had in his ability to help me find work. He had never seen me act, and I wasn't performing in anything at the time, except a line or two on an occasional television show. "When you're in a show, why don't you let me know," he said. "I can't really be of much help unless I see your work." I said I would be in touch and left. Even though nothing had come of it, I felt fine about our meeting. I'd had one more conversation, and every conversation made the next one a little more comfortable.

A few years went by, and I was in a play on Broadway that lasted only a couple of days, but on opening night, there was a man in a dark suit standing on the sidewalk as I came out of the stage door. "Hello," he said. "I'm Martin Bregman. I enjoyed your performance very much."

"Thanks," I said, or something just as memorable.

A year after that, I was finally starring in a play on Broadway. Diana Sands and I were in **The Owl and the Pussycat,** a two-character play that actually became sort of a hit. As I came out of the stage door on opening night, there he was again on the sidewalk.

"Martin Bregman. You did a wonderful job."

"Well, thank you." I was developing an incredible command of the English language.

Because of the play's surprising success, suddenly there were people interested in me. In one case, a little more interested than I would have liked. A few days after we opened, the phone rang and my agent told me I had a deal with the producer Ray Stark and his company Seven Arts. "I'm sorry," I said, "I have a deal?"

"It's pretty amazing," said the voice on the other end. "It's a deal for eight hundred thousand dollars."

I was a little disoriented by this. Arlene and I had only a few hundred dollars in the bank. "Eight **hundred thousand** dollars?"

"I'm sending over the papers."

I didn't understand what he meant by saying I had a deal. I had never heard there was an offer.

The papers came, and I read them with mounting anxiety. It was a seven-year deal. Two pictures a year. I could work for no other studio during those years. I would have to make whatever pictures they told me to make, wherever they wanted to shoot them. I would start at a few thousand a picture and get a raise every year, **if** they decided to keep me on for another year. They could drop me at any time. After I'd made fourteen pictures, I'd have been paid a total of eight hundred thousand dollars, which did sound like an enormous sum of money. A couple of years earlier, I had been driving a cab for twenty dollars a night or standing on the sidewalk until one in the morning, making a pocketful of change by parking cars in front of a fancy restaurant. But it was a **seven-year** contract, just the kind my father had suffered under at Warner Brothers. He was making only a couple of hundred a week, but in his first picture he made a sensational debut, playing George Gershwin in **Rhapsody in Blue.** The next picture they had for him, though, was a witless, low-budget musical. He tried to turn it down, and they reacted by putting him on suspension. You weren't allowed to turn down the studio in those days. There would be no income while he was on suspension, and he couldn't work for anyone else. He pleaded with his agent for help. A week later, the agent called him back.

"Don't worry, I smoothed it over."

"Thank God."

"No problem. All you have to do is report for work."

"Report for work?"

"Just do the musical and there won't be any more trouble."

He had no choice. The cheap musical was followed by smaller parts in gangster movies and even a horror movie. He never could hold out for better material. It was the tyranny of the old studio term contract. And I was holding in my hands the same contract, adjusted for inflation. It had already been signed by Ray Stark and was only waiting for my signature.

I called my agent, my voice shaking a little. "I don't think I want to do this," I said. "First of all, I live in New Jersey. What if they tell me I have to make fourteen pictures in Africa, or India, or California?" These were equally foreign places to me.

"You have to do it," he said. "We have a deal."

I was speechless. My agent, it turned out, had

been negotiating with Stark for six months and had agreed to this offer without once mentioning it to me.

I didn't know what to do. I felt inexperienced and alone. A powerful agent and a powerful producer had got together and decided what my life would be like for the next seven years. And they expected me to be excited about it. Dazed, I tried to get them to assure me that I wouldn't have to leave my family to make movies in remote places. They made some suggestions that sounded like a compromise, and I said that sounded better. In spite of the pressure they were applying, I tried not to say literally that I was agreeing to the deal. I was getting heartsick because they'd still be able to have me make whatever pictures they wanted.

In the middle of all this, I got a call from Bregman. Would I come up to his office and see him? Yes, sure, fine. When people asked for meetings, I went.

I got off the elevator on his floor. **He must be selling a** lot **of insurance**, I thought. Now, he had the whole floor. I went through two secretaries before I was shown into his office, which was approximately the size of a basketball court.

He was sitting on the corner of his desk. Not

a beige kidney this time, but dark, burnished wood. There was art on the walls and leather couches.

He smiled and congratulated me again on the play. And then he talked for what seemed like forty minutes about how I was going to have a really great life, and he'd like to be there. He had ideas. There were things he could suggest. He never really said anything specific. I actually didn't know what he was talking about. Finally, I said, "Well, thank you. I mean, I appreciate this. But—I really don't need any insurance."

He looked at me for ten long seconds. "Insurance. You think I'm selling you insurance?"

"I'm sorry, isn't that what you do?"

"I haven't sold insurance for years. I'm a business manager. Have you heard of Barbra Streisand?"

"Barbra Streisand? Yes. Sure."

"I manage her."

"You manage Barbra Streisand."

"That's right. If you need insurance, I can help you get some. But what I'd like to do is manage you."

I asked if I could think about it, and then I spent the next several minutes crossing the room to get to the door of his immense office.

Now I had something new to worry about. Having just been double-crossed by my agent, I was leery of letting someone else into my life who wanted to "manage" me. I talked about it with Arlene. She knew him as Marty. Her parents had known his parents for decades, and she had grown up with him. Only a few years older than her, he had been her baby-sitter when he was a teenager. They had grown up in the same building in the Bronx at 2911 Barnes Avenue.

As kids, she and Marty had both played in the courtyard between their two paired apartment buildings, the Mayflower and the Mayfair, where every family on every floor was known to them. They had friends in common and stories about all the neighbors, including Crazy Louis, a kid who would roam the building peeing into milk bottles left outside the tenants' doors.

Having grown up with a psychotic mother who blew hot one day and cold the next, I didn't trust people easily, but Arlene had known Marty for years, and he sounded like someone I could trust.

I called and told him I'd like to work with him, and we made a date to talk about it at lunch. We met at his office, and on the way out to the restaurant I noticed he was walking with a cane and a slight limp.

"Hurt your leg?" I asked him.

He looked at me sideways, as if I were making a bad joke. I realized I had never seen him walking. I'd seen him standing on a sidewalk, or sitting behind a desk, or on the edge of one. It was then, for the first time, that I found out he'd had polio as a boy. I'd had polio, too, but mine was mild. I wasn't left with paralysis. He clearly didn't want to talk about it, so at the restaurant we stuck to the contract I'd been offered.

"It's an awful lot of money," I told him.

"It's a lot of money if you think you won't have a career. But if they keep you on for fourteen pictures, you'll be worth much more than they're offering you now." In a way, he was suggesting patience. Steadfastness. Faith in myself.

I got Stark's people on the phone and told them I was definitely and finally turning down the deal. And they immediately sued. They claimed I had agreed personally to the offer. The moment on the phone when I carefully avoided saying more than a conditional statement that **if** I didn't have to travel too much it **might** be okay was, to them, a definite **yes.** They demanded that I fulfill the contract, **plus** pay them one hundred thousand dollars for some kind of damage I'd caused them. I didn't even have enough money to hire a lawyer without borrowing some.

I was called in to give my deposition. I sat in a lawyer's office and answered their questions, while out of the corner of my eye I saw a court stenographer's fingers tapping furiously, taking down everything I said. This was a seductive sight for an actor. I began to play a little to her, the way I would to a camera.

"Mr. Alda, your agents—aren't they authorized to negotiate for you?"

"Yes, but they can't make a deal, sir, without consulting me. They have to ask me first."

"But they do represent you in business, don't they?"

"They do, sir. But they do not represent me, sir, if I don't instruct them to."

I kept throwing in "sir" with my eye on the stenographer. I was trying to sound ironic—like the lawyers in the movies. Later, when I saw the transcript, I was crestfallen to see that she had left out every "sir." I sounded like a completely ordinary person instead of the orator from **Inherit the Wind** scathingly flinging out the honorifics.

Finally, our lawyer asked the court for a sum-mary judgment. That meant we'd go see a judge, let him look over the papers, and maybe he'd decide the case then and there without a long trial. We went downtown to the courthouse and were led into a small, cluttered office. A squat man who looked as if he should be playing the editor in a newspaper movie from the thirties took our documents from us and put on his reading glasses. He was in his shirtsleeves, and red galluses held up his trousers over a large belly. As he looked over their complaint, I thought of sections in it I had read so often that I knew them from memory. According to their document, I possessed "unique intellectual abilities." I was irreplaceable. They would suffer severe financial harm if I didn't fulfill the contract. The judge read for a few minutes, then looked up over his reading glasses and said, "Actors are so hard to find?" The lawyers for Seven Arts were a tough crew, but in that moment, I knew I had them. The judge found in our favor, and a couple of days later I was free of Ray Stark and in debt for six thousand dollars of lawyers' fees.

Eventually, a few more jobs came my way and our finances began to smooth out. In fact, the time had come, Marty felt, to incorporate myself for tax purposes. I had to choose a name for the new company. It wasn't much of a company, but its name seemed to have tremendous symbolic significance for me. I thought about it for days. "You have a name for the company yet?" our accountant would ask me at the end of every day.

"Not yet."

"We need a name."

Finally, I found one. It had been staring me in the face all along. It had been nine years since I had begun trying to find work as an actor. To scrape together a living during that time, I had been a cabdriver and a doorman; I'd colored baby pictures for a few cents an hour. I had been a waiter. I had sold mutual funds; I had gone to delicatessens and passed out twofers for Broadway shows. I had set up appointments to sell cheap jewelry in office buildings. All this, while making almost imperceptible progress each year toward a dim and hazy goal.

I called it the Patience Company.

I pictured a great, tall-masted ship making its way across an uncertain ocean toward an undiscovered land. Marty smiled when he heard the name, and a few days later, it wound up as an item in a gossip column: "This young actor is willing to take his time."

I was. I don't know where I got the sense to look at it this way. But I thought of everything in terms of the long haul. A few weeks before we got married, I started to backtrack and put Arlene through a difficult twenty-four hours of uncertainty—not because I was uncertain about loving her, but because I knew this was a decision that would affect us all our lives. It wasn't something we would ever turn away from. In the same way, I had hesitated in hooking up with Marty because I knew my relationships, even in business, were long-lasting.

But after we'd begun to work together, I began to notice a little tension between Marty and me. He had a strong personality, and so did I. What was worse, I had bridled under my father's controlling nature. Marty seemed to **thrive** on control. To get our finances in order, we had agreed to ask his permission for every purchase we made. Once, after I had gone to him and asked him if it was okay to buy a bicycle, I kept turning it over in my mind on the way home: **Why am I angry at him? I agreed to this.** The problem was that he had begun to stand in for my father. If we disagreed about politics, I couldn't let it be. The Vietnam War began to heat up, and our exchanges about it grew sharp. It's hard to find anyone now who thinks the Vietnam War was a good idea, but in those days, people were inflamed within seconds at the mention of the war. One day, we were standing in the middle of the floor in his office, angrily pointing fingers and yelling at each other. I blurted out, "Okay, fine. You've got a war. Now's your chance to go fight."

He stared at me for a moment, glaring. "No, now's **your** chance."

He held my gaze until I got it. I had forgotten his leg and the polio.

I was too embarrassed to apologize. I sat down and didn't bring up the war again with him.

Most of the time, though, we laughed together. He knew how to tell a funny story and could make me chuckle at some of my own youthful excesses. I had become fascinated with circadian rhythms, and I was amazed that a person's temperature varied several degrees during the day. I began carrying a thermometer around with me and recording my temperature every hour. Once in a meeting with him in his office, after I had stuck the thermometer in my mouth for the third time, he leaned forward and raised his voice about fifty-two decibels: "Are you nuts? Are you **nuts**? How am I going to get you a job if you walk in with that thing in your mouth?"

I would sit for hours with my feet up on his desk, figuring out strategies with him about how we'd get me my next job. Putting my feet on his desk, I suspect, was a way to defuse the power I felt he had over me. A few years later, acting in M*A*S*H, whenever I was in the colonel's office, my feet would wind up resting on his desk. My way of dealing with Marty became Hawkeye's way of dealing with authority.

After we'd been in business a long time, and I had outgrown some of my emotional immaturity, I was about to put my feet up on Marty's desk when I hesitated a moment and said, "Do you mind if I put my feet on your desk?"

He stared at me. "Now you ask me? **Now?** After twenty years of your feet on my desk? Now you ask me if you can put them there?"

I laughed, and I saw in that moment the patience he had. The immense patience. I understood how he could take months to romance a deal.

He had an even longer view than I did. When we made the contract for M*A*S*H, he asked for very little in salary, along with a small piece of the action. The studio was glad to agree because they almost never have to pay off on a share of profits. The unique bookkeeping practices in that part of the world do not anticipate that there will ever **be** any profit. And then they make sure there isn't any. Miraculously, they stay in business year after year without a dollar in profit. This is because they have a definition of profits that has no connection to anyone else's. When children run a lemonade stand, you hope that along with having fun, they come to understand the basic notion that when they subtract the cost of the lemons from the money they take in, what's left is a profit. It's a simple idea. You can say it without taking a second breath. The studio, on the other hand, had a "definition of profits" that was thirty pages long. You had to sign it and signify you agreed that everything they identified as a cost was in fact a cost. I read all thirty pages and realized there wasn't anything that didn't look like a lemon to them.

What they hadn't expected, though, was that the show would do so well that even under the terms of their crazy definition, there actually **would** be profits, and they had to share them.

That was probably the most important factor in my being able to have the professional life I've had after **M∗A∗S∗H**. I was able to do what interested me, to grow in my work, and to not take jobs just to pay the rent. Marty's skill at negotiating, and his wisdom about the long view, added something to my life I'd never have had without him.

And he was a master negotiator. He knew how to apply pressure to the other side without threatening an outcome he couldn't deliver. It would all be by indirection. Everything he did was by indirection. He'd call me on the phone and he'd be so indirect, I'd hang up the phone completely puzzled and Arlene would say, "What did he want?" and I'd say, "I don't know. Maybe he'll call back and tell me."

But applying pressure was his true art. Sometimes on our way into a meeting he'd say, "Let's do a Thomashefsky." Boris Thomashefsky was a great Yiddish actor from the nineteenth century, and when Marty said we should do a Thomashefsky, we would turn on the juice, and emotion would flow from our acting glands like borscht from a beet. In those moments, we weren't really negotiating; we were outraged at this threat to decency, justice, and the rights of humanity. The other side would usually become speechless.

With Marty I seemed to find my voice. Before we met, whenever a producer would try to steal from me or otherwise wrong me, I would become angry, and afraid of my anger, I would retreat into silence. In time, I developed an original but strange technique. I would suddenly begin speaking in a low, ominous tone. I would say enigmatically, "I can forgive or I can forget. Which would you like?" This would cause them to look at me oddly while they tried to figure out how, exactly, I could separate these two functions. No one ever expressed a preference for my forgiving or forgetting, but I think I sounded so crazy that they chose not to cross me anymore. With Marty, I learned the slow process of working with people until you had an agreement. And no matter what pressure he hinted at, he always worked with them.

Somehow, he did it without premeditation. He relied on inspiration; he improvised. Once, the day before an important meeting, I asked him what he was going to say. What was our plan, what line of talk would we pursue? "I don't know," he said impatiently. "I'll find out when we get there."

I found this a little unsettling, but no matter how uncertain I felt at times like that, he was always someone I could depend on. He made sure the agents were looking out for me; he marshaled the lawyers. He was the brains and the strength behind every deal we made. Working with him, I began to understand why heads of state have diplomats and why people who sell houses have real estate agents. If the two principals go head-to-head, there's no room to maneuver. Everything you say is your final word. It's more difficult to hint at disaster. And **hinting** at disaster, I discovered, is a much more powerful tool than threatening it. When Marty would tell a producer, "If you put that in the contract, you're going to have an unhappy actor," it was much more effective than telling the producer I would walk. Especially if he was arguing against a point in the contract that I would have lived with anyway.

Even after **M*A*S*H** had hit its stride, he still had the long view. Offers for movies weren't coming in; or if they were, they weren't very interesting. One of them was baffling. My agent took me out to dinner and gravely told me that a producer wanted me for an R-rated version of **The Taming of the Shrew**—which seemed to be heavy on rolling in the hay naked in iambic pentameter.

Marty and I decided I had to make my own film career. He encouraged me to work on a screenplay, and I began writing the script that three years later would turn out to be **The Se-**

181

duction of Joe Tynan. My working title was The Senator, but at the last minute, after the movie was shot and cut, the chairman of Universal Studios, Lew Wasserman, decided that there was too much sex in a movie centering on a U.S. senator. He was sure that if we called it The Senator, everyone would know that I was really writing about his friend Edward Kennedy. I hadn't been, but Wasserman was insistent. Marty and I delayed while I came up with lists of names that neither of us thought were any good. Finally, we wound up with just an hour or so to decide what the final title of the movie would be. We sat in the back of a car, tossing titles back and forth at each other, each one worse than the other. After a long silence, I said, "This guy is seduced by everything in his life. Money, sex, power. Let's call it The Seduction of Joe Tynan." We looked at each other blankly. It sounded like a completely stupid title, but we couldn't think of a better one.

The night the picture opened, I drove by a theater where it was playing. I got out of the car and walked up the block past hundreds of people standing in line to see one of the pictures playing in that theater. This is good. I thought. We can get their spillover when they sell out. I wondered what movie was doing so well. I asked someone in line, "What are you waiting to see?"

"We're waiting to see you."

Tynan was the first picture I'd written. We had made it for pennies, and it made the studio a lot of money. But it was a success, in part, for a reason I'd never have been able to predict. The research showed that 15 percent of the people who came to the theater came because of the word **seduction** in the title. Maybe the guy with iambic nudity had a point.

As we made movies, Marty and I were partners and made all our decisions together. Yet because I hadn't worked out my feelings for my father, I still smarted under what I thought of as Marty's controlling nature. Little things drove me crazy.

I would give him the first draft of a script that I had spent months on, and a couple of weeks later, I would get it back with little marks at the margins.

"What's this mean?" I asked.

"What?"

"This 'O.' The letter 'O' in the margin. What does 'O' mean?"

"That means omit."

That was it: omit. No explanation. No tender question, like "Do you really need this?" Just omit. I wanted to strangle him. But I called on patience and stuck it out. I might have left in a fit of righteous pique, the wounded author, but every time I came close to leaving, he softened and begged me to stay. He knew when to implore you and when to come at you with his guns blazing.

And he was usually right. Marty had produced, and was the driving force behind, a string of powerful movies. With films like **Serpico**, **Dog Day Afternoon**, and **Scarface**, he was becoming known as a tough bull of a producer, while I was becoming known as Sensitive Man. He was supposed to be the strong one. Yet there were times when we had to fire somebody, and he just couldn't do it. He couldn't even talk about it. He would tell me he'd take care of it, and the event would never take place. He simply couldn't fire someone. I would be the one who would walk into their office, explain why we had to let them go, and then lower the ax.

But he was no softy when he disagreed with you. Casting the movies was often painful because we both thought we knew best. It was at its worst when we'd cast a leading lady. He was certain that he, and only he, knew what sexy was.

We were friends and we always worked it out, but it took forever.

"Why can't we hire her? She's a terrific actress."

"Of course she's terrific. We need someone sexy for this."

"She's not sexy? Of course she's sexy."

"Please. I know sexy."

When my back would go up, he'd explain patiently, almost sweetly, "Look, we have an agreement. We can each veto a decision." It sounded so reasonable, so democratic. But when had we made such an agreement? Never. The agreement took place entirely in his head. On one picture, we kept vetoing each other's choices until we had turned down an entire generation of Hollywood's leading ladies.

But he didn't just know sexy, he knew acting. And in this case, he really knew it. He loved actors and respected them. Actors were a group of people toward whom he was exceptionally sensitive. When we were casting **The Four Seasons**, an enormously talented actor came in to see us. We needed someone for the part who was in good shape physically, and this actor looked as though he had started to put on weight. Marty casually asked him if he still worked out. "Oh, sure," he said, "all the time." Marty wanted to see him with his jacket off, but he couldn't bring himself to ask for something so embarrassing. As we chatted, Marty left the room to get a drink of water. It was a spring day, but for some reason, after a while, I noticed it was getting warm in the room. I thought, **The building should switch off the boilers for the warmer weather.** At one point, the temperature climbed to about eighty degrees, and the actor started to perspire. Finally, he couldn't stand the heat and took off his jacket. Marty turned to me with a look that said, **I knew it. He's out of shape.** We ended the meeting as all meetings like that end, full of pleasantries, and after the actor was gone, Marty went right back to studying his casting list. I said, "You know, it's good it got hot in here, or we'd never have known what shape he's in."

Marty didn't even look up from his papers. "While I was out of the room, I turned up the thermostat."

Slowly, I was resolving my feelings for my father, and in time, I learned to love the contradictions of the people who lived in Marty. He seemed sometimes to be sensitive, sometimes a tyrant, sometimes an artist, at times a hard businessman. He seemed able to be ethical, principled, relentless, and a cold-blooded softy all at once. Above all, he fought hard and loved deeply. And he was loyal.

I might never have known him this well or learned what I did from him if we hadn't stuck it out. He gave me a better sense of time. And time gave me a life I wouldn't have otherwise had.

In 2001, Marty's daughter, Marissa, was finishing high school, and she asked me to speak at her graduation. I was touched by that. Marty and his daughter adored each other, and when she was little, every time we took a plane someplace she thought I was taking him away from her. As we pulled off in a car once when she was five, she stuck her tongue out at me. She would never have remembered that moment, but when she asked me to speak at her commencement, I felt that somewhere in her heart she'd forgiven me.

During our time together, Marty and I have made good use of patience. But patience was more than a road to success. All by itself, patience gave some depth to my life. With patience, I could pause in my headlong rush and get a sense of where I was, who I was. Instead of racing from one thing to another, leaping across the surface like a frog jumping from one lily pad to another, I could dip down to where the roots, the values, were. All this was in my head when I got up to speak at Marissa's graduation.

A few years ago, the Internet was flooded with copies of a graduation speech the great writer Kurt Vonnegut had just given at MIT. It spread across the country in a few hours. It was quoted everywhere. I'd like to read some of it to you.

> Here are a few words for the class of 2001:
> Wear sunscreen.
> If I could offer you only one tip for the future, sunscreen would be it. The long-term benefits of sunscreen have been proved by scientists, whereas the rest of my advice has no basis more reliable than my own meandering experience. I will dispense this advice now.

Vonnegut went on to give them earnest advice—like: "Don't be reckless with other people's hearts. Don't put up with people who are reckless with yours."
He also urged them to "floss" and "stretch."

Be careful whose advice you buy.
Advice is a form of nostalgia.
Dispensing it is a way of fishing the
past from the disposal, wiping it off,
painting over the ugly parts, and
recycling it for more than it's worth.
But trust me on the sunscreen.

Now, the thing about this charming piece
by Kurt Vonnegut is that it wasn't written
by Kurt Vonnegut.

It was written by a newspaper
columnist in Chicago called Mary
Schmich. Some unknown person had
started sending it around as a speech by
Vonnegut. According to Schmich, "It went
to Italy and France, to Israel and Brazil, to
places I didn't know had electricity. Even
Mr. Vonnegut's wife, the photographer Jill
Krementz, received it, e-mailed it to several
friends, then asked her husband: Why
didn't you tell me you spoke at MIT? He
said: Because I didn't."

Somebody said it was one of the most
widely distributed pieces of e-mail in the
history of the Internet.

But after only a few hours of bouncing

around the world, it was identified as a hoax.

As soon as Vonnegut told a caller he hadn't written it, in a flash, the Internet was flooded with retractions. By the end of one extraordinary day, vast numbers of people had accepted and then rejected a worldwide hoax.

And that's what makes this Internet event a great image for the age in which we live. There are probably just as many lies going around now as ever before, but these days they're traveling at the speed of light. There are just as many people who want to fool you into thinking they've got it all figured out for you, but now you don't have nearly as much time to think it over.

And with the help of an engine for repetition that works on a scale unheard of in the past, the lies stick. People are still sending around the talk, thinking it was written by Vonnegut. I was sent a copy just last week.

It's a delightful piece of writing. But if it's presented as if it were by someone other than the person who wrote it, it steals that person's good name and gives itself a certain credibility before it has a chance to earn it honestly. So, as good as it is, it's a cheat. At least in the way it's offered to us.

So, you may be thinking, Big deal. It's just a few good jokes. But think about it . . . it could be selling you anything. It could be a cult religion that could separate you from friends and family, or a quack medicine that could leave you paralyzed, or bogus political information that causes you to elect a numbskull to the presidency.

God forbid.

Being able to know what's true and what's a lie is more urgently needed these days—and a lot harder to do—than ever before.

Now, more than ever, you need the wisdom of a trusted parent, partner, or friend to remind you of what counts. Now, more than ever, you need to know who you are and what you believe in.

Who you are is a tough one . . . because most of us have many people inside us. But in your finer moments you aspire to things that make sense in the long run. Even while you're enjoying a momentary distraction, somebody in you knows that down the road there's going to be something that will take some hard work. And that when it comes your way, you won't be able to wing it . . . you'll have to be prepared. That's the somebody who's the best and smartest you. That's the one who knows that the deepest pleasures come from learning how to do something difficult and that it's worth putting in the time to learn it.

Let yourself be all the yous you are, but don't let them crowd out the smart one.

As for what you believe in, your values really are not so much what you say as what you do. The more you bring those two things in line with each other, the easier it may be to get where you're going.

You may tell yourself you're going to Chicago, but it's hard to get to Chicago if you keep buying tickets to Las Vegas.

I think we don't realize how important time is. When we couldn't communicate at the speed of light, we probably didn't think about it that much.

But things do take time. Chemical reactions take time. Mourning a loss takes time. In fact, all the transitions in our lives take time. Getting in shape, physically or mentally, takes more than a weekend, no matter what they tell you in the brochure.

It takes time for a species to adapt to changes in the environment, and that's what makes us one of the most dangerous animals that ever lived. We can make changes in the environment that are so rapid that nature doesn't have time to replace the species we kill with others that are adapted to the alterations we've made in their habitats.

Now, although I think that knowing who you are and what you value and taking the time to look before you leap are all good ideas, that doesn't mean I know exactly how to do it. I don't want to kid you into thinking I've done it, it's a cinch. I'm still working on it, still trying to figure out how all this fits together. But this is what I aspire to. And I thought I'd pass it on.

So, as you make the transition from this page in your life to the next chapter . . . I wish you health, happiness, resilience, love, laughter, patience, cash, strength, smart friends, and plenty of time.

Maybe these few ideas will help start you on your way. I don't think it can do any harm to try them.

But if all else fails . . . floss, and wear your sunscreen.

Chapter 11

Winning the War on Winning

When I gave the eulogy for Vinegar, my grand-children's dead rabbit, I laid to rest something that had been gnawing impudently at my insides like Bugs Bunny on a carrot since I was a boy. Too often, I had needed to win, to come out of the game ahead—sometimes even if I wasn't in a game.

When I was eight, I would go with a friend on Saturdays to the Hitching Post Theatre on Holly-wood Boulevard to see a double feature of west-erns and serials. But my life had been changed the night before one of those Saturdays by seeing

Danny Kaye in **Up in Arms.** I had laughed so hard, I wanted to see it again and skip the westerns. My friend was reluctant to miss the serials at the Hitching Post. If we skipped a week of serials, we'd be lost in the continuing story and we'd never catch up. I didn't care. Danny Kaye thrilled me. I cajoled my friend for almost an hour with no results. Finally, I had a solution. I put a tin can on the sidewalk.

"Whoever kicks the can the farthest gets to pick the movie."

Tired of arguing, he agreed, and we each took a turn at kicking the tin can down the sidewalk. His kick went a good ten feet past mine. "Okay," I said. "That's fair. Let's make it the best two out of three."

He looked at me sideways. "And then we let the winner pick?"

"Right."

Bang. His kick landed the can ahead of mine. Again.

"Good," I said. "Three out of five."

"We just did two out of three."

"Three out of five. And that's it."

But that wasn't it, because the kid could just kick the hell out of a can. That didn't stop me, though. I went back to cajoling. At the end of the afternoon, we were still arguing and we never got to see any movie that day.

Two or three years later, I was embarked on winning with another boy my age. He was larger than me, but gentle and good-natured. He was Japanese, and a few years earlier, during the war, he had been interned in a camp. While he was living in barracks instead of the home where he was born, I was seeing war movies where the people who looked like me fought against people who looked like him. Inspired by the war movies, I liked to get into mock fights with him, and we would wrestle on the grass in front of my house. He didn't really want to wrestle, but in those days you made your own entertainment, and there wasn't much else to do. One day, I got him in an armlock, and after a moment, he let out a sound of pain. Instead of letting him go, I applied more pressure. In my mind, this wasn't real. We were in a movie. Having him under my control made me feel clever and powerful. When I did let him go, he looked at me with eyes that were focused like dark, flat disks.

"You hurt me."

It was then that I realized he had actually felt something. He wasn't just a prop in a movie. But that was only an early glimmer of my being able to understand that suffering could take place outside myself. It would be a long time before I could actually feel compassion. Meanwhile, I looked forward to winning and the sense of power it gave me. As good as power feels, it can lead to some regrettable actions. One of them is hard to think about, even now.

If I could go back and do it again, I would not have shot my pet rabbits dead when I was eleven years old. I was only a boy, and I didn't understand what those three ear-splitting minutes would be like, but it has stuck with me ever since.

For reasons I can't remember now, my parents allowed me to have a .22-caliber rifle. It was long and slim, with a weighty heft. It made a solid clicking sound when you worked the pump action. Uncle Frank, my mother's brother, lived with us and worked at teaching me to respect the gun.

It was one of the few things he worked at. A strike that lasted nine months had put him out of his job as a carpenter at Warner Brothers, and he never was able to get other work. He said it was because no one would hire a man who had been in jail. He had been arrested as a young man for passing counterfeit money and jailed for a few weeks. He told me one morning, as he stirred his coffee slowly, that he had taken the rap for his wife's brother and had suffered for it ever since.

Uncle Frank was in his late thirties when he came to live with us. My father, who was acting in movies at the studio, managed to get him the first job my uncle had held in years. He had a broom of white hair and the easy manner of an older person, and he spoke in a language of the street I'd never heard before. He once made a loan to someone he'd just met: "I taken a liking to him," he said, "so I turned around and handed him a three spot." He was a decent person, but I was never really sure he would have preferred going to work every day to sitting at home dreaming and telling stories. His imagination was vivid to him. He could become excited to the point of losing his voice when talking about panning for gold. He invited me to help him build a sluice box for washing gold-bearing gravel out of a riverbed, although I don't remember his ever actually using it, since there was no evidence that the gravel contained any gold.

But he did work at training me to respect the rifle. He would sit with me in the evening, solemnly taking it apart, reaming out the barrel, and rubbing the inner parts with gauze and sweet-smelling oil until they shone.

During the day, I would roam the eleven-acre ranch where we lived and the mountains that ringed it, looking for things to shoot at. I liked the idea of hunting, although the thought of eating a dead wild animal repelled me. I was attracted to the idea of aiming at things and, if possible, killing them, the way they did in the war movies. The soldiers in those films didn't **eat** the dead Germans and Japanese, they just killed them and then laughed and congratulated one another. It seemed like an agreeable way to pass the time.

But I never was able to sneak up on anything expertly enough to get off a shot at it. Once, at dusk, I was with Uncle Frank up by the stable. The pungent smell of eucalyptus wafted up from the dead leaves under our feet as we walked over to where I heard birds chattering. They had collected in the tall trees for the evening. If only I could scare them off their perches, I'd have some targets to fire at. I started throwing rocks up into the branches. The birds weren't budging, so I tried larger rocks. Finally, I picked up a stone the size of a small brick and threw it straight up, watching where it went.

Where it went was straight back at my face. It split my lip and pushed my front tooth back into my mouth. Uncle Frank put his thumb and index finger in there and eased the tooth back into place, telling me not to worry, it would be all right.

In the dark, we walked back down the gravel road to the house as I bled. I was worried about what my mother would think. She was excitable. Actually, she was more than excitable—she was schizophrenic and paranoid. But I didn't know that then. I just knew she reacted to even ordinary things in a big way. When we came into the kitchen, she saw me covered with blood, saw her brother holding the gun, and screamed, "My God, you've shot him!"

Frank was angry with her. "Jo! Will you stop? You always think the worst."

She screamed back at him, and they argued for a while while I dripped onto the floor; then they put ice on my face. Later in the week, a dentist cut into my gum and removed the root of the tooth where it had broken off. He took out the dead nerve and bleached the tooth, but eventually it turned blue, and I had to keep having it bleached every few years. I was losing parts of my own body in pursuit of the hunt, but that seemed to be the extent of the damage I caused. Until the afternoon of the rabbits.

I had been given a couple of white bunnies as

an Easter gift. Uncle Frank and I built cages, where I would stand and observe them for hours. They had a habit that, at eleven, I found fascinating. The male would hop onto the female and jitter rapidly for a minute or so, and then he would fall over on his side as if he were dead. It would take him a good ten minutes to come back to life. Then a few weeks later, there would be more rabbits. It went on like that until there were twelve of them. We were busy building cages. But within a few months, disease hit them, an infection that made their ears swell to three times their size. I felt sorry for the animals because it seemed to me they were in pain. I was tearful when we called in a vet and he said there was nothing he could do for them. They'd have to be destroyed.

But then my eleven-year-old brain made one of those decisions that seem so much better at the time than they do a few minutes later. **They have to die,** I thought, **so why not shoot them?** I could put them out of their misery **and** have a chance to kill something. I told Uncle Frank what I wanted to do, and he didn't discourage me. He even helped me take them out of their cages and put them on the ground. I still wonder why he didn't warn me about what might happen. Maybe he couldn't foresee it, either.

The rabbits stood on a patch of dry land, hardly moving except for the twitching of their noses as they sniffed at the dusty dirt. I raised the rifle, took aim, and began firing. I wasn't prepared for what the force of the bullets would do to them. They flew up into the air and flopped back onto the ground. Some didn't die right away, and I had to shoot at them again. I was missing them completely or just wounding them. As the bullets hit the arid ground, a small cloud rose up. I was shocked at what I saw through the haze of dust and fear, but once I'd wounded them, I had to keep going. Rabbits have no voice, but they were making a squealing sound that made me cringe. I was frightened, and I began to cry. I wanted it to be over, but the more I pulled the trigger, the worse my aim was and the more damage I caused. Finally, they were dead and the dust settled. The rabbits lay still on the bloodied ground. I handed the rifle to my uncle. Neither of us spoke.

That night, we sat at a small wooden table in the rumpus room and I watched him clean the rifle as he always did: emptying the ammunition, swabbing the barrel, cleaning and oiling the action. Then he reloaded it. I watched as each bullet went in. Then he put on the safety and handed it to me.

I carried the rifle upstairs and laid it on the top deck of my bunk bed. A few minutes later, after brushing my teeth, I looked at the rifle and tried to remember if my uncle had loaded it. I had watched him, but I couldn't recall. I was pretty sure it wasn't loaded, but I wanted to be certain, and I chose the worst way to find out. I undid the safety, pointed the rifle at the ceiling, and pulled the trigger, expecting to hear an empty click. Instead there was a bang, and I was staring at a hole in the ceiling. **Oh, my God,** I thought, my heart pounding. I stared at the hole for what seemed like minutes, and then I paced the room, telling myself I didn't just do this stupid thing. But every time I looked up, there was the hole in the ceiling.

I went downstairs and told my parents what had happened. They hadn't heard the noise, but I could tell from the deadly calm in the way they received my news that I had just done something monumentally bad. They took the gun and said that Uncle Frank would make sure the bullets were removed safely and told me to go back to bed and not dwell on it.

Upstairs, as I lay in bed, I stared at the hole in the ceiling and couldn't sleep. Finally I got up and, standing on the top bunk, stuffed some toilet paper in the hole. The wad of paper remained there for the rest of my childhood, but I never saw the gun again. It just disappeared from the house.

The memory of the rabbits never really went away. Like the hole in the ceiling, it simply got plugged up for a while. Years later, when I was old enough to attract the attention of the army, the experience with the rabbits came back to me— not consciously, but through a sharp pain in my back muscles. I didn't like killing things anymore, and it seemed that in the army reserve, where I was learning how to be an officer, all they seemed to want to talk about was killing people. I was given the job of teaching recruits the most efficient way to kill the greatest number of people with a single mortar round. I tried my best to accommodate my superior officers. I studied up on mortars and gave it everything I had, telling jokes to keep the students' attention and simplifying the material so they'd remember it. I sent them away with several good tips on how to destroy at least a dozen people with one round; then I went home and doubled up in cramps. Soon, every time I put on my uniform, the tissue under my shoulder blades, just over my lungs, would seize up. Once, when I picked up the uniform at the dry cleaners, I got only halfway down the block before I couldn't walk without stopping every few feet to lean against a building, squinting in pain.

I was sent to Georgia to complete my education as a military hero, and once there, I was given a rifle again. "This is your rifle," our sergeant said. "Your rifle is your friend. Take care of it, and it will take care of you." He actually said things like that. I learned how to clean it and take it apart blindfolded and was careful never, ever, to let it stand with the muzzle in the dirt. I was trying hard to be friends with it.

One morning before dawn, we marched to the firing range. I was sleepy but kind of excited. We would be aiming at targets, not at anything living, and I did enjoy shooting. I settled happily onto the ground on my stomach, the sharp pebbles poking into my starched fatigues. I adjusted the rifle's strap over my cocked elbow at the approved angle, and I sighted down the barrel.

"Ready on the right! Ready on the left! Commence . . . firing!"

I curled my finger over the trigger—squeezing, not pulling it—and, after correcting for windage, I began blowing holes in the paper targets.

A hundred other young soldiers were going

through the same motions, and as a result, there was so much noise that I almost didn't hear the sergeant call for cease-fire. Then there was silence on the firing line—except that something over on my left was giving off a piercing, high-pitched sound. After a while, I realized the sound was coming from inside my left ear. I wiggled my finger in the ear, but the steady ringing tone didn't go away.

I heard it for the next three days, and when it finally did subside, I had to keep asking people what they had just said. I had become partially deaf in the left ear, and not so good on the right side, either. After a while, when it was clear that my hearing wasn't coming back, I began to feel there was a real downside to gunpowder.

As I got older, my thoughts were influenced even more by the afternoon with the rabbits. I began to mistrust the feeling of power that came from the need to win between me and people who were close to me.

A friend asked me to lunch to give him advice. His marriage was about to break up because his wife thought he loved gambling more than her. Winning, even just the chance of winning, made him rush off to Vegas or Santa Anita. And when they argued about it at night in their bedroom, he had to win there, too. He looked truly confused.

"What should I do?"

"I don't know. I'm starting to think there are times when the only way to win is by losing."

"How does that work?"

"Surrender to her."

"I should just give in?"

"No, surrender."

"That means giving in."

"No. Look. The song doesn't say, 'I give in, dear.' It says, 'I **surrender, dear.**'"

I was talking as if I had the answer to his problem, but I was a lot of battles away from being able to surrender—to give myself freely to someone I loved. I'd had three chances in my life to learn how to do it: with my wife, my children, and my grandchildren. And each time I learned how to do it, I had to start all over from scratch with the next batch.

Finally, on a day I spent with two of my grandchildren, I began to feel I was getting the hang of it once and for all. I should have known it would be a significant day for me because it involved another dead rabbit. What is it with rabbits? I wonder. Why do they come into my life every time I have a big change? I used to bite

their chunky chocolate ears off at Easter time before I ate their hollow bodies. Is this why they
keep following me?

There's a time, I think, as we get older when
we need the company of youth. They let us be
young again; they let us have a do-over on things
we missed the first time. I craved the company of
my grandchildren when they came along and
would have been happy if I could have made myself indispensable to them. This wasn't surren-
dering to them, of course, but wanting them to
surrender to me. There was a talk we had one
day, though, when things clicked. It was Satur-
day, May 27, 2006. I made a note of it because it
was a perfect day.

Livvie and Izzy, two of our granddaughters
who were living down the street at the time,
called in the morning and asked if they could
visit. I had something else to do, but I decided to
drop it for them. Livvie was nine and Izzy was
eleven, and we cooked a breakfast together big
enough for ten people. We made pancakes and
waffles and oatmeal; then, when we were full and
couldn't eat any more, they said they wanted to
make something, so we looked in my closet for
shoes that we could make something out of. Livvie found a pair of tan walking shoes, and Izzy

found garish tennis shoes with lots of red and blue glitz all over them. I found two old telephones in a closet, and we took them apart. Then we made holes in the shoes and ran wires into them and installed the phones under the leather tongues. We plugged the other end of the wires into phone jacks, and the girls made phone calls with the shoes held to their ears.

I drove them home because they wanted to get back to show off their new phones, but when we got there, we heard from Teo, their six-year-old brother, that their baby rabbit had died. They'd found him in the grass the day before, hungry and weak. His mother had been killed by a fox, and only her feet had remained. They had scooped up the baby, named him Vinegar, and kept him safe in a box. But he seemed to be in shock, not eating or even moving. Then, while we were making the phones, he died.

Izzy and Livvie laid Vinegar's body in a small cardboard box. They got a shovel and started digging a grave under a tree. Everyone was surprisingly good-humored about the burial. As they dug, I said it was too bad Vinegar didn't have a sister, because then her name could be Olive Oil. They thought that was pretty funny. Then, to let them have a chance to reflect on their feelings for the animal, I spoke a few words in the way of a eulogy for Vinegar.

"He was a good little rabbit. And we're sorry he's gone. He was with us for a while, and now he's going back into the earth. Ashes to ashes and dust to dust."

Izzy looked at me, puzzled. "What's that mean about ashes?"

"They used to say that at funerals. It means that we sort of came from the earth, and now our bodies go back to the earth and become dust again."

Izzy thought about that for a while. "You know, Grandpa, it's really sad that you know something like that."

We chalked inscriptions on the driveway, saying good-bye to Vinegar. Before I left for my house, I wrote a short note in chalk and ended it: "I love you, Vinegar. Love, Olive." I was hoping that the balm of love might take away some of the sting of death.

They called me an hour later from their shoe phones, and their voices sounded surprisingly clear, considering they were speaking through layers of shoelaces and bereavement. They wanted to bike over and make notepad holders for the phones. They thought we could construct them from sliced-up tennis balls. I said sure, but I was worried about their biking across the main road. I said I'd come pick them up.

"No, we're **fine**. We won't get hurt."

The fantasy of biking to Grandma and Grandpa's house was driving any possibility of harm from their minds. I had to decide how strict I'd be. I could press them on it and win, or I could let them have the pleasure of the wind in their face, their leg muscles pumping, as they made their own way.

I backed off as much as I could. "Would you please think about **walking** your bikes across the road? Because that would make me feel much better."

They said okay, but in such an offhand way that I was sure they wouldn't bother. I didn't press them on it. I surrendered to their enthusiasm, which was all sweetness and bubbles.

They came over, and we cut up tennis balls and put notepads in them, and we made plans for making phones out of teddy bears and whatever else we could find. We would sell them at yard sales or online—none of which we ever did, but our dreams were happy ones.

At the end of the day, as I watched from the porch, they climbed on their bikes and started down the driveway toward home. After a few feet, they stopped and turned toward me.

"Oh, by the way, Grandpa?"

"Yes?"

"We took your tips on crossing the road."

I smiled as they turned and pumped their bikes out to the road.

And that was the meaning of life **that** day.

Chapter 12

Pass the Plate, Mr. Feynman

I was four, maybe five. My mother had a small gold watch that she left on her vanity one morning. A vanity, in those days, was a table you sat at while you made up your face, reflected in three mirrors. Her table was covered with boxes of powders, lipsticks, eyelash curlers, and eyebrow pencils. Sometimes, curious to see what would happen, I would mix some of the powders together with toothpaste, hoping for a fizz or maybe even a small explosion. But what drew me to the table this day was the watch. I wondered how it worked. What was inside that made the hands go around? I took it from the table in my short fingers and pulled at it. I shook it and pulled at it again. Amazingly, the back came off, and there were the little round things going in circles, ticking and clicking. It was a wonderful sight. After I watched it for a while, I put the back of the watch in place again, but it wouldn't stay. I couldn't get it to clamp on. I knew I couldn't leave it on the table in pieces like this, so I put it between my teeth and bit down on it. That held the watch together. I put it back on the table and went to my toy box.

Sometime later, my mother came over to where I was playing and began talking to me in a tone of voice I recognized as fake casual. I knew something was up. She was a terrible actress, and if she was acting this casual, something bad must be about to happen.

"Allie, I'm going to ask you something, and I want you to tell me the truth. Have you been playing with my watch?"

"Your watch?"

"If you tell me the truth, I won't punish you."

Why would she punish me? This was not good. My lip started to twitch. I had that sinking feeling of doom where something bulges in the back of your throat and heads for your stomach with menace.

"I think you were playing with my watch. I found tooth marks on it. Did you . . . now, tell me the truth . . ." She paused delicately. "Did you bite my watch?"

Of course I didn't bite her watch. I reassembled it. I applied pressure to it. I wasn't stupid enough to eat a watch. None of this came out of my mouth, because I didn't possess these words then. Instead, tears came to my eyes and I nodded. She forgave me, and we moved on. After that, I tended not to fix things with my teeth, but my curiosity didn't diminish. It might even have grown stronger.

Curiosity had the power to engage me completely. It sent me to a zone where time stopped and I floated through that infinite space between dots on the face of a watch. Curiosity could make me feel more alive.

I lived with a father who sometimes was absent, off acting somewhere for long stretches, and with a mother who was there in every way except for her mind, which was diseased. While I sidestepped her paranoia and tried to outguess her schizophrenia, I was alone, and although there was a lot of laughter in the house when it was full of people, much of the time I had to invent my own entertainment. I didn't mind it then, and I'm grateful now for the solitude that was the soil in which my curiosity could grow.

The days I spent in the California mountains where we lived, isolated from other people, had a sun-washed emptiness about them, but excitement swelled in me when I went out exploring them. I worked my way through the mountain trails and through the yards of books on our living room shelves that held strange stories and odd characters. When I couldn't understand what I saw or read, I experimented with my own explanations. Sometimes I just lay on my back, looking at the clouds, figuring out what shapes they were trying to become.

Allowing this childish curiosity to continue on through my whole life has given me satisfaction and maybe even a sense of meaning. It stimulates a part of my brain that registers pleasure; and whether it has meaning or not, it feels as though it does. No matter how old I get, I have the feeling that if I can keep this curiosity flame lit, I'll see the world in a way that never gets stale. Life will have a taste that delights. Maybe that isn't actual meaning or purpose, but somehow it sets that worry aside. And I don't want to lose it.

I listen more intently now when I hear about older people who are learning things they'll never use but which they learn for the sheer pleasure of taking in something new. A friend told me her mother, at ninety-six, was reading all of Lincoln's speeches because she wanted to learn more about him as a writer. She was doing this not to write about Lincoln or make some other use of it, but rather for the pleasure of following her curiosity, wherever it led. Another friend told me about his mother, who, at close to one hundred, was still riding the bus around Los Angeles. He was concerned for her safety and asked why she did this. She said, "Because I meet so many interesting people."

Their curiosity gives them pleasure; it puts gas in their tank. But more than that, it leads them to places they never expected to see and enables them to accomplish things that surprise them and satisfy them.

On **Scientific American Frontiers,** the science program I did for eleven years, I kept meeting people who studied things simply because they were interesting. I stood one day on the sandy shore of Lake Michigan in Chicago with two scientists who were fascinated with why the water squishes away from your footprint when you walk on the beach, or why coffee stains always form into rings on a countertop. From these simple questions, they were learning about how materials interact with one another. A universe was opening up to them by studying ordinary things that at first seemed trivial.

Paying attention to the apparently trivial intrigued me. Doors were opening up to me that might have forever remained closed if I hadn't paid attention to the small things that didn't seem to matter. It was as though a key to the big city could be found in pieces of chewing gum stuck to the sidewalk. That was an idea as valuable as it was strange.

This may have been what led me to Feynman's plate. At a tricky point in his life, the great physicist Richard Feynman became interested in a plate—an ordinary dinner plate—and, in a way, it changed his life. At a tricky point in **my** life, I became interested in Feynman, so the plate flew off the page from Feynman's hands into mine.

It was a time when I was ready for something new, but I didn't exactly know what it was. M*A*S*H had come to an end, to a great extent because I had felt we should end it on a high point. I had pretty much decided I didn't want to write and direct movies for a while, in this case because there was beginning to be a noticeable roominess in the theaters where my movies were being shown. I was free now to do what interested me, not because it was a career move, but simply because it interested me. I was following my curiosity, and I was looking for fun.

I was asked to become the host of **Scientific American Frontiers**, and I jumped at it—but only if I could interview the scientists myself.

I found this new life liberating. And it was probably why I reacted so strongly to Feynman's plate.

I came across the story of the plate in a collection of autobiographical stories called **Surely You're Joking, Mr. Feynman!** and I became infatuated with this man who possessed such a brilliant mind—some people said a mind second to Einstein's—yet had such an extraordinary capacity to entertain and to present himself as just an ordinary guy. His total honesty and his unwillingness to fool himself or others made him a hero of mine.

I wanted to imitate his way of thinking, and at one point I studied his trick of finding square roots in an instant. I was able to do it for a day or two, but because it's not something I need to come up with very often, I soon forgot how to do it. Then I saw an experiment in one of his books I couldn't resist. He told a story of how he had become interested in the idea that dogs had such an acute sense of smell that it made him wonder if people had that same sense, but perhaps not as well developed. He wondered if we could exploit a similar sense. So he asked a group of friends to stand by a bookcase, and when he left the room one of them was to take one book off the shelf and then put it back. He left, and when he came back, he methodically smelled everyone's hands. Then he put his nose to the bookcase and ran it along the shelves. Within a couple of minutes, he didn't know why or how he had done it, but he identified the book that had been handled.

I couldn't compare brains with Feynman, but I could compare noses. I was on vacation with my grandchildren, and we went to a sitting room in our hotel where there was a little library for the guests. I told them that after I left the room, I wanted them to take a book from the shelf, open it up, look inside, and then put it back. Then I left. When I came back, they were smiling, knowing I couldn't possibly pick the right book out of two hundred of them. I smelled their hands—then I applied my nose to the shelf, just as Feynman had. I scanned the shelves two or three times. But nothing seemed to be happening. I had a sensation in my nose—a vague rumor of an aroma—but I couldn't quite smell it on the books. Finally, there was one book I thought I'd have a go with. It kept registering with me every time my nose passed it on the shelf. I pointed at the book.

"Is it this one?"

There was a long pause.

"No. It's the book right next to it."

I took that as a major victory and never repeated the experiment. Feynman may have been my hero, but I didn't yet possess his heroic desire to prove myself wrong.

I kept reading everything I could about him, and one day I came across a book that revealed his character so charmingly, I got excited about the idea of playing him on the stage. You may hope to be realistic as a person, but when you're an actor, somewhere in the back of your head you're thinking, **I'm not as smart as Feynman or as wise as Feynman, but for two hours a night, I can be Feynman,** and you jump on it.

It was astonishingly difficult, though, to get Feynman boxed within the confines of a play. He was a man of so many parts, no matter how you told the story there was always an arm or a leg sticking out of the box. We went through more drafts than I've ever seen a play go through. We became discouraged many times, missing an opening date we'd scheduled at least once and twice almost canceling the play altogether. It was frustrating to know we had one of the world's great characters, yet we couldn't create an evening in which he could come alive on the stage. Peter Parnell wrote draft after draft. And they were all vastly different. He tried to come at Feynman from every conceivable angle. Some writers will turn in a second draft that differs from the first only in that some of the punctuation has been rethought. Peter would write an entirely new play with a whole new set of characters, covering entirely different parts of Feynman's life. Then, after we read it aloud and discussed it for a day or two, he would throw it out and write a new Feynman play.

It was a maddening process, but finally we were getting ready to open for a run in Los Angeles. We did a preview performance for students and professors from Caltech in Pasadena. Feynman had spent the last decades of his life teaching at Caltech and was beloved there, and we were laying our hearts on the table to show them the play we had devised about their legend.

The theater was packed with young scientists who knew him better than we did, but they got

223

so caught up in our imaginary Feynman that at one point when I asked a hypothetical question about science, somebody raised his hand and tried to give his answer. The evening was so filled with the thunder of their laughter and the emotion they felt for their hero, we wondered if we'd ever have a night like that again. But we did. We ran for six months in Los Angeles and then played for a season in New York. The theater was full every night, and over the course of our run about fifty thousand people were introduced to Richard Feynman.

Between the closing in Los Angeles and the New York opening, the attack of 9/11 occurred. We played in New York to an audience completely different from the one we'd been accustomed to. As I came out onstage opening night at Lincoln Center, the attack was only three weeks behind us and Ground Zero just a few dozen blocks from us. At one point in the play, Feynman tells the audience about his experience working on the first atomic bomb at Los Alamos. He describes the sight of the white blast in the desert and his subsequent depression months later. He tells of sitting in a New York restaurant and calculating the destruction spreading out from where he was if the bomb were to go off there, putting him at ground zero. The response from the audience was the most complete stillness I've ever heard in a theater. A few months earlier in Los Angeles, audiences had been drawn in, fascinated, by this story of a man who had helped create the most destructive device ever built, but now they were hearing an account not only of their past, but of their possible future. There was a sense of unity and clarity of thought— a thread that ran from Feynman, to Peter Parnell, to me, to the audience, and back to Feynman; it was a sensation I had never known on a stage before.

The audience had changed. And, through playing Feynman, I was changing, too.

Because I had interviewed scientists on television for eleven years and then played Feynman, my name was beginning to be associated, in a way, with science. I didn't mind this for two reasons. First, one of my flaws, which I consider charming, is that I don't mind appearing smarter than I am. Second, I had learned early in life to make the best use of whatever comes my way. It was how I knew what to work on and sometimes even how I found out who I was. So when I was invited places to talk about science, or help in some way to promote an interest in science, I began to see that I could use this lifelong interest as a way to be helpful. It was tricky, because I wanted to be helpful, but I also knew I was in so far over my head, my hat was floating a mile above me.

A year or so after we opened **QED,** I was asked to give the commencement talk at Caltech. I said yes immediately, and immediately, I was terrified. I was still apparently looking for ways to scare myself. I didn't mind it if people thought I was smarter than I was. But I didn't really want to show them in public how wrong they were. I agonized over the speech for months. I tried out ideas on friends, and I would watch their faces for signs of interest or, more likely, simple confusion.

Finally, I decided simply to tell the story of my infatuation with Feynman and the maddening effort of trying to figure out who he was and to get that person on the stage. It was difficult partly because it was so hard to understand his work in quantum mechanics, but it was difficult also because of the complex person he was. Everything we tried diminished him to just one aspect of an ordinary guy. And as much as he wanted to present himself as an ordinary guy, he was as far from ordinary as you can get. As one writer said in the title of a book about Feynman, he was "no ordinary genius."

So on a sunny day in 2002, I drove to Caltech, climbed the steps to the rostrum, and looked out over the faces of several thousand people seated in a long esplanade in front of me, many of them graduating with degrees in science. I had come a long way since the days when, shooting M*A*S*H, I had been idly curious about the very place where I was standing.

Twenty-five or thirty years ago, on my days off from the Korean War, which was at that time being waged at Twentieth Century–Fox in Beverly Hills, I would often come to Pasadena to visit the Rembrandts at the Norton Simon Museum or take a walk in the Huntington Gardens. And sometimes I would drive by Caltech and give it a glance and wonder what interesting stuff was going on in there. I had been reading about science avidly for years, and I was immensely curious about how scientists went about what they did. It didn't occur to me each time I passed by that there was one particular man in one of these buildings who at that moment might be drawing gluon tubes on a blackboard, or playing the bongos, or just standing

227

looking out the window as a young woman passed by—a man in whom, in a few years, I would become intensely interested.

One day exactly twenty-eight years ago, he was standing right here, giving the commencement address. (This is the way the universe operates. First Richard Feynman gives the talk; then twenty-eight years later, an actor who played him on the stage gives it. This is what's called entropy. This is what happens just before the cosmos reaches a temperature of absolute zero.)

Let me tell you a little about the path that led me here. After I had read several books about Richard Feynman, I brought one of them, a charming, touching book by Ralph Leighton called Tuva or Bust!, to Gordon Davidson at the Mark Taper Forum in Los Angeles. I wondered if he thought we might be able to make a play about Feynman. He suggested Peter Parnell to write the play, and the three of us started off on a journey to find out who Richard Feynman was. We thought we'd open the play a year or so later. Instead, it took us over six years.

We had no idea how hard it would be.

For one thing, Feynman was an extremely unusual person. Toward the end of his life, he knew he was dying and he knew exactly what the most important questions were, and he knew he had a shot at answering them . . . yet he kept to his habit of doing only what interested him.

He spent a good part of his time trying to get to this little place in the middle of Asia called Tuva, mainly because its capital was spelled with no vowels, which for some reason he found extremely interesting.

But just as getting to Tuva was tantalizingly difficult for Feynman, getting to Feynman became maddeningly hard for us.

What part of him do you focus on? He helped create the atomic bomb, he helped figure out why the Challenger blew up, he understood the most puzzling questions in physics so deeply, they gave him the Nobel Prize. Which facet of him do you let catch the most light? The one who was a revered teacher, a bongo player, an artist, a hilarious raconteur, or a safecracker?

We wanted to make a play about Feynman, but which Feynman?

A mathematician friend of mine suggested that a central image for a play about him could be Feynman's own idea of a sum over histories. Just as Feynman saw a photon taking every possible path on its way to your eye, Feynman himself took every possible path on his way through life. He was the sum of all his histories.

Well, nature may be smart enough to know how to average all the paths of a photon. But we three theater people couldn't figure out how to add up all the histories that made up Feynman.

At one point, I said, "You know what we ought to do? We ought to write a play about three guys sitting around in a hotel room, trying to figure out a play about Feynman. They never figure it out. They just drive themselves crazy."

We researched him like mad, of course. The people who knew him and worked with him and loved him here at Caltech opened their doors and their hearts to us. They were extremely generous and helpful as we struggled to reduce this irreducible person to an evening in the theater.

I think one of the things I most hoped

would come through was his honesty. He never wanted to deceive anyone, especially himself. He questioned his every assumption. And when he was talking to ordinary people with no training in physics, he never fell back on his authority as a great thinker. He felt that if he couldn't say it in everyday words, he probably didn't understand it himself.

I was fascinated by this in him. He knew more than most of us will ever know, yet he insisted on speaking our language.

Like Dante in his time, he could say the most exquisitely subtle things in the language of the common people. He was an American genius, and like many American artists, he was direct and colloquial . . . not afraid to take a look at the ordinary and not afraid to go deeply into it to reveal the extraordinary roots of ordinary things.

And yet he recoiled from oversimplification. He wasn't interested in dumbing down science . . . he was looking for clarity.

If he left something out, he always told you what he was leaving out, so you didn't get a false picture of a simplicity that wasn't there. And later, when things got more complex, you were prepared for it.

It may not seem important exactly how Feynman achieved clarity. Maybe we should just be glad he did it and let it go at that. But I think it is important. Because I think we have to figure out how we can do it, too.

For one thing, we live in a time when massive means of destruction are right here in our hands. We're probably the first species capable of doing this much damage to our planet. We can make the birds stop singing; we can still the fish and make the insects fall from the trees like black rain. And ironically, we've been brought here by reason, by rationality. We cannot afford to live in a culture that doesn't use the power in its hands with the kind of rationality that produced it in the first place.

But right now, instead of reason, a lot of people are making use of wishes, dreams, mantras, and incantations. They're trying to heal themselves using crystals, magnets, and herbs with unknown properties. People will offer you a pill made from the leaf of an obscure plant and say, "Take it, it can't hurt you, it's natural." But so is deadly nightshade.

Interestingly, they expect the plant to have active properties to cure them, but they're certain it has no active properties that can harm them. How do they know that?

I mention this not to denigrate anyone's beliefs (I feel strongly that we're all entitled to our beliefs, just as we're entitled to our feelings), but I bring it up to point out that we're in a culture that increasingly holds that science is just another belief.

And I guess it's easier to believe something . . . anything . . . than not to know.

We don't like uncertainty—so we gravitate back to the last comfortable solution we had—no matter how cockeyed it is.

But Feynman was comfortable with not knowing. He enjoyed it. He would proceed for a while with an idea as if he believed it was the answer. But that was only a temporary belief in order to allow himself to follow it wherever it led. Then, a little while later, he would vigorously attack the idea to see if it could stand up to every test he could think of. If it couldn't stand up, then he simply decided he just didn't know. "Not knowing," he said, "is much more interesting than believing an answer which might be wrong."

You're graduating today partly as Feynman's heirs in this gloriously courageous willingness to be unsure. And just as he was heir to Newton, who was in turn heir to Galileo . . . I hope you'll think about devoting some time to helping the rest of us become your heirs.

I'm assuming you're here at Caltech because you love science, and I'm assuming you've learned a great deal here about how to do science. I'm asking you today to devote some significant part of your life to figuring out how to share your love of science with the rest of us.

But not just because explaining to us what you do will get you more funding for what you do . . . although it surely will . . . but just because you love what you do.

And while you're explaining it,

remember that dazzling us with jargon might make us sit in awe of your work, but it won't make us love it.

Tell us frankly how you got there. If you got there by many twists and turns and blind alleys, don't leave that out. We love a detective story. If you enjoyed the adventure of getting there, so will we.

Most scientists do leave that out. By the time we hear about their great discoveries, a lot of the doubt is gone. The mistakes and wrong turns are left out . . . and it doesn't sound like a human thing they've done. It separates us from the process.

Whatever you do, help us love science the way you do.

Like the young man so head over heels about his sweetheart, he can't stop talking about her; like the young woman so in love with her young man, she wants everyone to know how wonderful he is . . . show us pictures, tell us stories, make us crave to meet your beloved.

Don't just tell us science is good for us and, therefore, we ought to fund you for it; don't tell us to trust you that your fancy words actually mean something; don't keep the tricks of your trade up an elite sleeve. Don't be merchants, or mandarins, or magicians . . . be lovers!

Look, we're accustomed in our culture to know when a commercial is coming. We know how to turn it off. But love we can't resist.

You may be swayed by people who insist they're only interested in hearing about the practical applications of science. You may be tempted to bend over backward, telling them what they want to hear.

When Feynman stood here and spoke twenty-eight years ago, he cautioned scientists against going too far in telling laypeople about the wonderful everyday applications of their work, especially if there weren't any. I don't think Feynman needed to justify his curiosity about nature. Pure science was pure pleasure. It was fun.

It's like the story of the plate.

The one thing I was certain of from the beginning was that we had to have the story of the plate in the play. It was central. The author, Peter Parnell, would do draft after draft. And I would look at it and say, "Where's the plate?" I drove him crazy.

The plate story is this: After the war, Feynman became depressed. His first wife had just died of tuberculosis, and the realization of the awful destructive power of the bomb he had helped make had finally sunk in. He was teaching at Cornell, but he had no taste for it. He couldn't concentrate. Then, one day, he's in the school cafeteria and some guy starts fooling around, tossing a plate in the air. Feynman watches the design on the rim of the plate as it spins, and he sees that as it spins, the plate wobbles. He gets fascinated, and he tries to figure out the relationship between the spin and the wobble. He spends months on this and finally comes up with this complicated equation, which he shows to Hans Bethe.

And Bethe says, "That's interesting, Feynman, but what's the importance of it?"

And Feynman says, "It has no importance, it's just fun!"

But, see, that's the thing—it not only brought him out of his slump, but that playful inquiry, according to Feynman, eventually led in a circuitous way to the work that won him the Nobel Prize.

But no matter where it might have led

him, he made up his mind that day in the cafeteria never to work on anything that didn't interest him, that wasn't fun.

Of course, what Feynman was looking for was serious fun. It was the awe he felt when he looked at nature. And not just the official great wonders of nature, but any little part of nature, because any little part of it is as amazing and beautiful and complicated as the whole thing is.

So, this is interesting. I'm urging you to be like someone whom I admit I've found to be pretty elusive.

Here I am, seven years later. And just as Feynman never got to see Tuva, I never really found Feynman. Not really. I came close; but he was too many things. He had too many histories.

We came up with a play in QED that was immensely satisfying. It was beautifully written and beautifully directed, and it gave the audience a Feynman that was as close an approximation as we could come up with. But part of me feels that a large chunk of the man is still beyond our reach—probably beyond the reach of anyone. He's just out of sight, smiling at us. Laughing at how he put one over on us, letting us think he was just an ordinary guy. A guy we could get.

It turns out, though, that the old thing about the destination not being as valuable as the journey really is true.

Because when we began, finding Feynman seemed important, and I guess it was . . . but as it turned out, looking for Feynman has been the fun.

Every once in a while, though, I can feel Feynman looking over my shoulder, and he's not smiling. Like right now. I'm at the end of my talk, and I feel the pressure of the words he closed his talk with twenty-eight years ago. "One last piece of advice," he said. "Never say you'll give a talk unless you know clearly what you're going to talk about and more or less what you're going to say."

In other words, where are the brass tacks?

I had been looking for something I could offer these young scientists that was more useful than admiration. And it was through playing Feynman that I found it. Feynman and I were light-years apart, but two things we shared were curiosity and a desire to see science communicated clearly. I took a chance and challenged them.

Okay, let me be more or less practical. I'm going to propose something to you today. I realize it's a childish idea, something only an unschooled layperson would come up with, but it's specific enough that it might get you thinking.

What if each of you decided to take just one thing you love about science and, no matter how complicated it is, figure out how to make it understood by a million people? There are about five hundred of you taking part in this ceremony today. If just a few of you were successful, that would make several million people a lot smarter.

How you do it is up to you. You're clever people, and I bet you'll come up with some ingenious solutions. On the other hand, you may be thinking, Why? Why should I do this impossible thing?

Well, I don't know, maybe for the same reason that the birds sing.

If it does for you what it does for birds, there's a lot to recommend it:

1. It's a good way to improve your chances of having sex.
2. It feels good to sing.
3. Singing is the music nature makes when it dances the dance of life.

You are the universe announcing itself to itself. You open your mouth, and a little muscle in your throat makes a corner of nature vibrate. You're one part of the forest saying, "This is what I think I know," while another part of the forest is saying, "Yeah? Well, this is what I think I know!" Your chirpings are the harmony of all knowledge.

You've studied how nature works. Is there anything more beautiful than that? Is there anything greater to sing about?

So sing.

Sing out.

Sing.

Out.

Thank you, and good luck.

I wonder if they knew how much I envied them. My curiosity helped me feel alive—it kept a spring in my step—but they could make their curiosity work for them. The spring in **their** step could let them bound tall buildings.

They could look inside a universe so much more complicated than my mother's watch. How could I not envy them? They could see the wheels spinning and figure out what made the hands turn—and they knew how to get the cover back on without using their teeth.

Chapter 13

As Friends Go . . .

As I watched him from the wings, there was one point in the play when he behaved with such passion that I thought he was possessed by something out of his control. I had seen comic actors take off in a moment of improvisation, but I had never seen this kind of inspired anger and overwhelming strength. I stood next to the house curtain ropes and watched that event every night for most of a year and wished I could become him. Ossie Davis was a big man, and kind; he taught Sunday school; he was gentle with children and courteous to strangers. He wrote a play that for all its contempt for racial injustice was a rollicking comedy. But when he became aroused in anger near the end of the play, it could stop your breathing. That he had that much fury on the stage and yet was so gentle in life were the two best reasons to want to be like him.

I met Ossie in my early twenties when I acted in his play **Purlie Victorious,** and we saw each other on and off over the next few decades. He sometimes sent me a script he had written, generously asking if I had any comments. With all his talent and skill, he was always humble. Humble and funny. He came to see me when I did a one-man show and kidded me that I finally had a part in which I could talk as much as I wanted; and then at dinner afterward, he made a toast to me that brought tears to my eyes. His heart was as full as his laugh. In the sixties, his wisdom, his dignity, and his courage during the civil rights movement had helped pull America from the thorny bramble of hatred and set it back where it belonged on the road to equality. He was a big, granite monument of a man and a sweet candy bar of a friend.

And then he was dead.

He died suddenly, on a film shoot. His heart just gave out. I got a call that Ruby was inviting me to speak at his funeral service, and I was touched that she had thought of me. As I thought about what I would say, I realized that a moment like this is a small test of what a life means. When the person is gone and all that's left of someone you've loved is the body, how do you call him back? Is it by reciting his accomplishments? I couldn't forget what Ossie had achieved, but I found myself remembering him better and more pungently in his simplest, most human moments. Those were the moments when his life came up against mine and made it better.

His funeral was on February 12, 2005. Those of us who had been asked to speak met in a small room at the back of the Riverside Church in New York City. There were people there from all parts of Ossie's life: actors, politicians, civil rights leaders. We chatted for a while, as you do at a funeral, in an odd combination of sadness and laughter, and then we took our places in a pew at the front of the great Gothic cathedral. One by one, Ossie's friends got up to speak, except for Wynton Marsalis, who simply played his horn as he paced slowly at the front of the congregation. Then it was my turn.

Ossie was my hero, and he still is. He was my friend, and I loved him for forty-four

years. And the day he died, I had a reaction I'm sure many of us had—I didn't believe it. Somehow, I had thought that his grace, his laughter, his everlasting smile, were all so alive that they would always be with us.

But a hero doesn't die if the people he touched remember the ways in which he touched them. When I was twenty-five, I stood in the wings every night watching Ossie in Purlie Victorious; it was one of the ways I learned how to act. His power and his spontaneity were so vivid that it made the hair rise on your neck, and you thought you were looking at someone who was being struck by lightning. Forty-four years later, I still aspire to what Ossie had, and I hope that I can have just a little bit of Ossie in me.

I learned many things from Ossie and Ruby. When we shot the movie version of Purlie, they taught me how to eat sweet-potato pie. They did. They said, "You take a bite, and then you go like this: uhn—uhn—uhn." And I still do that—not just with sweet-potato pie, but with a plate of pasta, too. And every time I go like that, I think of Ossie and Ruby, and I love them again.

As a writer, he mixed laughter and pain and the longings of all humanity. As a citizen, he brought all of those longings off the stage to help resolve them in our own lives. I love him for his laughter and his kindness. I love him for his service to his country—a country that with all the honors it gave him never could give him what he gave to his country. He gave a rich, deep voice to all our longings for simple brotherhood. He gave us pride in ourselves, no matter what part of the earth we sprang from. "I find in being black a thing of beauty," I heard him say every night in Purlie. "A native land in every Negro face," he said. Ossie was a thing of beauty, a native land for everyone whose heart aches for justice and compassion. He spoke of black princes—he was one.

His was the power of decency, the power of art, the power of intelligence and love, and sometimes the power of righteous anger. If we're decent and artful and smart, and we let ourselves love and be angry at injustice, then Ossie—that beautiful black prince—will never die. I love you, Ossie.

A tape of the service was broadcast on stations all over the country. Ossie's death was a national event. People stopped me in airports thousands of miles away from New York to tell me they'd seen his memorial on television. They wanted to talk about how much Ossie had meant to them. A day or so after the service, Peter Jennings and his wife, Kayce, were over for dinner, and as we sat down at the table, a rebroadcast of the service was coming over a local channel. Peter hadn't been at the ceremony and wanted to see a few minutes of it. We stood and watched it on the kitchen television. My talk came on the air, and then a few minutes later, Bill Clinton spoke. Through the lens of the television camera, you could see two very different styles. We both had strong feelings for Ossie, but my words had been chosen; his words seemed to come to him on the spot—without hesitation. You could hear the people in the church responding to his spontaneity. His simple, unaffected presence was exactly what I'd always admired in Ossie's acting.

As we walked back to the table, Peter said to me, "You were very good. . . ." He paused. "But Clinton was **great**." And he was.

We smiled and sat down to eat, neither of us

aware that within seven months I would be speaking at Peter's memorial.

Peter died August 7, 2005, from lung cancer. His illness shocked people all around the country and even his friends, who weren't prepared for how swiftly the illness had ravaged him.

But even while Peter was still fighting for his life, I lost a third friend in the same year. In June, Anne Bancroft died of cancer of the uterus.

I first met Anne when we were kids. I was in college at Fordham. I was nineteen, beginning my senior year, and because I loved to perform and was unafraid to get up in front of a crowd, I was asked to emcee a football rally. It didn't bother me that I had no interest in football and couldn't even pronounce the coach's Polish name. I liked the idea of getting a crowd to its feet, roaring with energy. I didn't even mind that I got a laugh when I mangled the coach's name. All I knew then was the fun of their cheers. But when I introduced Anne and she came out onstage, I heard what cheers could sound like. She was four years older than me and had just come back to the Bronx after a couple of years in Hollywood learning the trade of the starlet. Going through the motions of the Good-Looking Girl from New York probably irritated her, because she was a serious actress, but someone in the senior class had asked her to help out at the rally, and she gamely played the part. She came onstage with a smile as big as the Bronx itself and an armful of roses that she tossed, one by one, into the audience. With each rose that was tossed, the screams of joy that swelled from the testosterone-soaked crowd in the gymnasium was deafening. Fordham was an all-male school at the time, and you saw women only on the way there in the subway. Women were an underground interest, and Anne made the ground shake like the A train.

A few years later, Anne married Mel Brooks, and a couple of decades later, when we had all become successful enough to vacation every year on the same island in the Caribbean, we became friends. I came to understand that the sources of some of her best acting were her own deeply felt passions. Anne had a volatile temper that she could spring on you with no warning. She was a Vesuvius of emotion, and watching her erupt, I was inspired to write the part of the incendiary Italian woman in **The Four Seasons.** Rita Moreno played the part in the movie brilliantly, and I can't think of anyone else playing it, but it was Anne who made me laugh first at the character.

The picture was about friendship, but I didn't fully understand what I had written until after I'd shot and edited the movie and had to go out and talk about it to the press. This was clearly a case of finding out what you think after you've written it. Finally, I saw that this was a story of the four seasons of friendship: spring, where everyone is fresh and attractive and new to one another; summer, where the glare of the sun begins to show everyone's blemishes; autumn, where the fig leaves finally fall and you see who they really are; and the winter of friendship, where you either drop them and start all over again with another springtime set of friends or take them as they are and huddle against the cold winds of aging.

At dinner one night, having written the part with Anne in mind, I asked her to play it in the movie. I think we were just moving from the springtime of our friendship and heading into summer. I didn't know her well enough to realize that she'd be offended by my asking to have dinner with her without warning her that I was going to bring up business. I probably was too afraid she'd turn me down to bring it up in advance, but it was a mistake. Her reaction was an immediate lack of interest; in fact, I saw a little puff of smoke warning of an eruption, but I had only myself to blame.

I don't know if she ever saw the movie, and if she did, if she recognized any of herself in it. Some of my other friends saw themselves in characters that had nothing to do with them. After the movie came out, I had to have several dinners explaining that characters with similar professions or hobbies didn't always mean I was writing about my actual friends.

We wound up shooting some of the movie on St. John, where we had vacationed with Anne and Mel for thirty years and where Anne befriended our children and then our grandchildren. It was where I saw the woman under the actress; the girl who was born to Michael and Millie Italiano, whom they named Anna Maria Louisa. Theaters all over Broadway dimmed their lights for her when she died, but that was a gesture to the actress and star. It was the person at the white-hot core of the star that I remembered when she was gone.

On July 1, Mel took over the St. James Theatre on West Forty-fourth Street. The memorial was held in a theater, I suppose, to honor her career, but he invited only a couple of hundred people who had actually known her well. Mel wanted a private service, a personal time of re-membering, and when I got up to speak, that's what I wanted, too.

Today, as we celebrate the life of Anne Bancroft, I want to make sure we also remember the life of Anna Maria Louisa Italiano. I miss Anne; and even more, I miss Anna Maria Louisa, the Italian kid from the Bronx.

As an actress, Anne often spoke in a way that conveyed an air of sophistication and worldly learning, but in private she never lost the tones and inflections of the scrappy, passionate, loving kid from the Bronx. It wasn't just that she never forgot who she was; she never left who she was. Anna Maria Louisa grew, as Anne, in her art and in her understanding of herself and of all of the people she played, but she never stopped being the Italiano girl.

She was a practical idealist. She didn't make speeches about the rights of women. Instead, she hired women for jobs that went traditionally to men, like the director of photography of the film she directed.

I never heard her make lofty statements

about loving humanity; she was more focused than that. My children and grandchildren all have memories of her that are intimate, specific moments, moments when she related to them on a simple, direct level. On vacation, she sat and admired sea glass with them, and they responded by searching for sea glass for her for days. She put them in touch with nature, not with a lecture, but with her genuine, human curiosity and love of beauty.

She didn't just admire nature; she put her fingers in it and rearranged it. She loved the sea. She loved to swim in it and rummage around by the shore, and she could take seashells that were beautiful in themselves and transform them into objects of art.

She fought her last battle with the same passion and scrappiness and creativity she brought to all the rest of her life. When the time came to cover her head, she knitted hats that were marvelous inventions of texture and color.

Anne Bancroft was a beloved actress. And I celebrate her. And I celebrate the

**woman inside her all those years and who
made her who she was: I celebrate Anna
Maria Louisa Italiano.**

A few years before she died, Anne and Mel
bought a house near where we lived in the country. We knew they loved jazz, so we took them
one night to hear a concert played by some of the
great jazz musicians at Peter Jennings's house.
Peter held the concert every year to raise money
for a nearby community center. He was always
quietly and instinctively generous to people who
could use a hand. In the streets of the big city, he
felt it was the most natural thing in the world,
not merely to give a homeless person some
money, but to talk to him, to ask about his life,
or just to see how he was doing. Peter went to a
soup kitchen regularly, not to make an appear-
ance, but to ladle out soup to people who were
hungry.

Peter and I had met as neighbors twenty
years earlier and had slowly built a warm friendship. He was exacting in his work, anchoring the
news, and he could be frank in his assessment of
everything else he saw around him. One day, he
and I were talking on his porch when he felt I
had said something politically partisan and a lit-

tle too heated. "I didn't realize you were an ideologue," he said.

"Well, I don't think I am."

"Well, yes, I'm sorry to say, you are. I'll tell you—last time you were here, you had a little too much to drink. You were much looser about things."

"I was?"

"Yes, and I think I like you better drunk."

You couldn't get mad at him because whatever he told you was honestly intended to make you a better person. And it would, if you listened to it.

We visited him again on a summer day on that porch a couple of weeks before the end. He was thin and weak, but gracious—determined to stand and greet us. He joked with us and looked with great care at the book of photographs we brought him, telling us he was going to study it after we'd left. After talking quietly with us for half an hour, he told us we'd better go; he was losing his strength. We gave him a hug and never saw him again.

He had loved music, all kinds of music. There was a gospel choir at his memorial and a performance by Yo-Yo Ma. We heard the Royal Canadian Mounted Police Honor Guard; a New

York Police Department bagpiper; and, again, a soulful piece by Wynton Marsalis.

Peter had given a new tone to broadcast news, and it grew out of his own voice, out of who he was as a person. That was what I remembered about him that day.

When things go wrong on television, we get snow. When the signal can't reach us, when mountains interfere, we get a fuzzy, chaotic blizzard of electronic noise. When the signal does reach us, of course, then the real challenge begins: to put something on the screen that's better than snow. Peter Jennings melted the snow with warmth, intelligence, and grace.

When Peter was your friend, he cared about how you were doing. He made sure you heard about things that affected your life. And this was how tens of millions of people who never met him felt.

I think so many people responded to him the way they did because Peter was a truly authentic person. He was who he was, even though he was many things at once. He was complex and simple at the same time. Knowledgeable and

inquisitive. Kind and tough. All at the same time.

He was gracious, yet he was direct, too. Once after dinner at our house, he stayed after the others had left and washed the dishes with us. We couldn't talk him out of it. He did it naturally and without fanfare; gracefully. Then he turned to me while he was drying a dish and said, "Now that everyone's gone, if I were you, I'd send the wine back to where you bought it. It's a little off." Graceful and yet direct.

He was personally courageous and self-sustaining, yet he cared about the homeless, the hungry, and the excluded as if he took it for granted that it was his responsibility to lend a hand.

He never preached. In fact, I never really knew what his political thoughts were, but he was excited about ideas and different ways of looking at things, and he was just as excited about passing those ideas on to others. I don't think I ever left his house without his giving me a book to read.

The last book he gave me was a copy of the U.S. Constitution. A little pocket-sized book. He said he carried it with him wherever he went, and he urged me to carry it and to take it out and read it whenever I was waiting someplace and had a few minutes. "You'll learn a lot," he said.

I kept it on my bed table. But when we lost him, I began carrying it with me, as he had asked me to.

I took the small book out of my pocket and opened it.

I was reading it the other day, and my eye caught this phrase:

"Article II, Section 2, Clause 3: The President shall have Power to fill up all Vacancies that may happen during the Recess of the Senate. . . ."

I stopped and thought about that phrase for a moment.

There is a vacancy now that no president, no one on earth, has the power to fill. Others will step in and do his job with excellence, but no one can replace the unique person who was Peter. All of us around the country who felt he was a friend we could count on—we're left now with just a bit of snow on the screen.

If I could say one last thing to Peter, it would be to say to him the last thing he said to all of us on his final broadcast:
Dear friend, I'd say . . .
"Thanks. And good night."

I held back some emotion, put the Constitution in my pocket, and moved down the aisle quickly. I missed what the other speakers said because I had only a few minutes to get to a live radio broadcast. I knew Peter would have understood.

So what do I make of all this? What was I saying to myself in these talks? Three of my friends who happened to be well known died within the same year, and I spoke about each of them in public. It's true that who they were to the rest of the world was a part of what they were to me, but it wasn't what I missed, what I longed for, in them.

What made their lives count to me most were very small moments. This, it seems to me, is what a life adds up to: the sight of one of them hunching over seashells with my grandchild, or roughly kidding me out of taking myself seriously, or teaching me three musical notes in appreciation of sweet-potato pie.

I can see Ossie smiling at me. We're on the set of the movie version of **Purlie.** I can see the chunk of pie in my hand, and I can taste it. And Ossie says, "Go like this. You take a bite, and then you go unh, unh, **unh.**" Each sound is a different note on a minor scale, a thread of blue notes signifying pleasure.

I make the sound, and you know what? It makes the pie taste better. That's the short way to say what all three of my friends meant to me. They made the pie taste better.

Chapter 14

Taking the Wider Way

"Just give it a try," my father said. "That's all I'm asking."

It was spring, and the pale green of the leaves would turn soon into the saturated lushness of a summer of freedom. I didn't want to spend it in a darkened classroom, learning something I would never use. I knew my father had wanted to be a doctor when he was young, and I was pretty sure that was why he was urging me to look into medicine. I didn't want any part of it. I was morbidly depressed by the idea that instead of making people laugh, I might have to spend my life touching sick people and looking at blood. But he begged me to take a summer course in chemistry—a premed requirement—just to see if I might like it, he said.

There wasn't much chance that I'd like it. With two friends, I had just written a musical comedy in high school and played one of the leading parts. I had my sights set on show business, and I was nervous, thinking I was setting out on a path that might lead to the operating theater instead of the 46th Street Theatre.

And besides, I thought, **I'm not interested in this stuff. I want to be an artist.** I didn't realize it, but I was turning away from something that I would eventually wish I'd learned.

When I was a boy, I had loved science. I was an amateur inventor. I was always doing experiments; always trying to figure out how things got the way they were. I would rummage around in a neighbor's garage looking for metal rods and little electric motors that I could use to build my inventions. But then I started high school—not long before C. P. Snow delivered his lecture at Cambridge about the two cultures: the culture of art and the culture of science. He talked about how they had moved apart and had become largely ignorant of each other.

I didn't know it at the time, but Snow was describing me. In high school, I started to believe that if you loved art, you couldn't love science. Soon after I decided to be an artist, I started pulling back from science. I was perfectly primed for falling in love with the Romantic poets in college. The Romantics hated getting and spending and went into ecstasies over daffodils. But they also mistrusted science. Science, they felt, chops everything up into equations; it dices up nature and kills it.

I thought so, too, and I didn't want to spend my summer studying chemistry. But my father was humble about the way he asked me to just consider it, and I couldn't turn him down.

One day in early summer, I stepped out of the warmth of the sun and walked into a huge amphitheater in a Gothic building on the Fordham campus in the Bronx. I entered at the back, and as I adjusted my eyes to the dim light, I saw rows of seats descending in a semicircle down to a platform where a thin professor started flinging out words I couldn't understand. He pointed at the blackboard. "What's the valence?" he cried out. People called out numbers, and he scribbled furiously and unintelligibly with his chalk. The only time I had ever heard the word **valence** used before had to do with curtains hanging in a window. Unless I had accidentally walked into a summer course in interior decorating, I was going to have a language problem here. I had arrived on time, but somehow they all seemed to be in the middle of something. Abstruse terms were flying at me like dive-bombers. I never had the faintest idea what the professor was talking about. I barely got it that molecules were made up of atoms that somehow were stuck together. I had no idea that electrons were involved. Afraid that this was what the rest of my life was going to be like, I decided to do my best to fail the course. Actually, I didn't have to work all that hard at it. I failed the final exam spectacularly. My father, in his gentle way, took the news without a show of disappointment. "Well, at least you tried," he said.

But I hadn't.

Many times since then, I've wished that I had been able to bridge Snow's cultural divide in those early days and learn the languages of chemistry and mathematics, which is probably the closest we can come to the language of nature itself. I never did. I regained my youthful curiosity and tried to know more about what those languages described, but it was a haphazard process. My eleven years interviewing scientists on **Scientific**

American Frontiers brought me closer to understanding how scientists think. Still, much of the language and many of the concepts of science were foreign to me, as they are to most of us. Over the centuries, like continental drift, the landmasses of science and the humanities, once united in an Eden called Pangaea, had separated and developed their own intellectual flora and fauna, becoming home to mutually alien species of thought. Where once those interested in humanity could mix freely with those interested in the **rest** of nature, now an ocean of strangeness separated us.

I was gripped by this thought, and before long it developed into a kind of hobby. Whenever I was asked to talk before a group of scientists, I would ask them to find ways to drag those continents back together somehow. In a way, it was an odd hobby for somebody who got a score of ten in his final chemistry exam—but when you think about it, what's a better example of the problem?

Fifty-five years after I'd hesitatingly entered the darkened amphitheater in the Bronx, I was walking up the path of the entrance to Rockefeller University on New York's East Side, on my way to give one of those talks I had no business giving, and again, I was as excited as I was scared.

Paul Nurse, president of Rockefeller, came out to meet me and give me a welcoming hug. Paul is a Nobel Prize winner in physiology/medicine and one of those rare people who know how scientists think and how the rest of us think and can speak the language of both with nuance and humor. Paul introduced me warmly to the audience, but as I got up to speak, I was a little too aware that he probably wasn't the only Nobelist in the audience and that I was in even further over my head than usual. I had been nervously rewriting the talk until the last second and hadn't had time to read it out loud even once. I usually slip into the men's room before a talk and stand in one of the stalls, trying rapidly to say most of it from memory, but it was too late for that. As I spoke, I noticed I was gripped by a low-grade panic that produced a slight stutter that I hoped would be taken as charming spontaneity. It came out, of course, like a stutter. This was something like the anxiety most of us feel when we come up against science—an encounter that often has all the trappings of a blind date. Which was exactly what I was there to talk about.

Think of it—a blind date: a meeting set up between two strangers with low expectations and high anxiety. Will I be stuck with this person the whole night?— Should I have had a friend call and tell me my grandmother's in the emergency room? **And, at the same time, they may be thinking,** Maybe this is the person who can save my life. **All this has the same false hope, wariness, and anxiety as when a lot of the public makes a glancing, brief encounter with science.**

Blind dates have a history of occasionally turning into disasters, and so do our anxious dates with science.

In 1991 in Texas, they started digging a tunnel that would be twelve feet wide and run in a circle fifty-four miles long. They were going to install in this tunnel a series of very high-powered magnets, each weighing tons. The magnets would pull along protons faster and faster until they came very close to the speed of light. Then the protons would smash into each other, momentarily creating particles, many of which had never been observed before. This was going to be the biggest, most

sophisticated particle accelerator ever built, and we were going to make real progress in discovering the origin of matter. We were going to understand reality in a way we never had before. Congress thought about it, and of course they already understand reality in a way no one ever has. After they'd spent almost two billion dollars on the accelerator, they canceled it—because it might cost as much as eleven billion, and that was too much, they felt, to spend on knowledge that had no practical application. Senator Dale Bumpers said, "It would be nice to know the origin of matter. It would be even nicer to have a balanced budget."

One way or another, pure basic research almost always leads to practical results, but at first, new knowledge often appears trivial; a luxury.

We haven't progressed much beyond where we were in 1745 when Pieter van Musschenbroek in the town of Leyden figured out the Leyden jar and stored large amounts of electric charge in it. It was a novelty to most people. And a few years later, Benjamin Franklin called lightning down a wire on a silk kite during a thunderstorm and stored it in a Leyden jar. Everyone was startled by this amazing phenomenon of electricity, but still they felt it was essentially just a parlor trick. They didn't know then that the great parlor trick to come would be the little box in the parlor that brought the farthest reaches of the world to the other end of the carpet, and that the leaders of the world would rise and fall based on their performance in that little box, no bigger than a Leyden jar.

Here's an update on the fate of the superconducting supercollider. The site has been vacant since the project was canceled. But there is still a tunnel underground. This August, a Dallas firm, called the Collider Data Center, started renting out the tunnel as a place to store computer data.

The giant circle in the ground will house magnetic disks with old bookkeeping records sitting on them, instead of giant magnets hurtling protons at nearly the speed of light and slamming them together to produce bursts of new knowledge. The

death of the possible at the hands of the practical.

There are plenty of examples of missed opportunities and even actual disasters caused by the lack of good communication of science. At Rockefeller, I mentioned the devastation caused in 2004 by the tsunami in the Indian Ocean. People on the coasts of the Indian Ocean had not been trained by newspaper articles or radio shows to understand the danger of tsunamis. They weren't aware of the significance of an early warning sign like a beach draining rapidly. There were even people who stood and watched the tidal wave rolling in, completely unaware that it was a wall of death. Over two hundred thousand people were lost, and most of them could have been saved if an early warning system had been in place.

But the greatest disaster in the communication of science, I guess, could turn out to be global warming; and the problem is not just people's understanding of it, but their very ability to understand it. We still have a poor grasp of how science works. When research contradicts a

271

previous finding, it sounds as though scientists can't make up their minds. Peer review sounds like bickering. We don't really get it that weighing evidence is different from taking on a belief. Someone told me once that he believed in chaos theory. I didn't really know what he meant, but apparently he felt that you could accept it or not, based on how it struck you; how it felt.

As long as most of us don't understand how scientists think, then self-serving politicians can label the work of respected researchers "junk science." How can we help people know the difference between junk science and junk politics?

Maybe it won't be so bad. Maybe global warming won't turn out to be a disaster unlike any we've faced since we've been on the planet. We've lived through a small ice age; maybe we can live through another of the great extinctions.

But even if it turns out to be nowhere near that bad—if all we had to face was the world's oceans moving inland a little, chasing people out of their homes—the economic impact would be huge.

Ten percent of the world's population lives near the ocean at an elevation of less than thirty-three feet above sea level. If the Greenland ice sheet were to melt, it's estimated the oceans would rise twenty-one feet. Even a three-foot rise would swamp cities all along the eastern seaboard. A six-foot rise would put most of Florida underwater. This all sounds so catastrophic that it's almost impossible to hear it without a voice in our head saying, This can't be. Somebody has to check these figures. That's exactly what I wish we could get the public to do: check the figures. We're shooting craps in a game where we've bet our house and home and have no idea what the odds are.

We've got to move on from this blind date. We can't excommunicate ourselves from science—we need, not just to make people aware of natural disasters, but to avoid the greater catastrophe of the death of knowledge itself.

At the same time that science is approaching the very peaks of the Himalayas of scientific understanding, down in the valleys, we live among the greatest number of people ever alive who believe in magic. As one astronomer has pointed out, there is a daily column in almost every newspaper on astrology and barely an occasional article on astronomy.

Critical thinking and a respect for evidence seem to be dwindling.

You may remember a year or so ago when Nicholas Kristof reported in The New York Times that a Gallup poll had shown that forty-eight percent of Americans believe in creationism, and only twenty-eight percent in evolution (most of the rest aren't sure or lean toward creationism). . . . He said that Americans are more than twice as likely to believe in the devil as in evolution. Sixty-eight percent believe in the devil and twenty-eight percent in evolution.

How about this: If you go to www.afterlifetelegrams.com, you'll read this exciting offer:

"For a donation of five dollars per word (five-word minimum), we can have telegrams delivered to people who have passed away." This is done with the help of terminally ill volunteers who memorize the telegrams before passing away, and then they deliver the telegrams after they have passed away.

We have a lot of work to do.

This has been going on for a long time, of course. By the time technology was fresh and the Luddites rose from their sleep, roaming the countryside like a band of zombies, smashing looms—by the time that poets, intoxicated with romance, said that science was cold and blind to the poetry of nature—the stage was set, the scenery was up, for a tragic play. Art and science would be antagonists, where before they had been lovers.

It's been nearly fifty years since C. P. Snow noticed this fissure in our cultural brain. And in too many ways it's still with us, as though the corpus callosum uniting our hemispheres has been severed and each side speaks a language neither can understand without a translator. I want to see us bring those hemispheres back into communication again. I want to see those lovers reunited. They were made for each other.

So, what can we do?

I've spent my life trying to be an artist,

so my approach to this problem may sound a little off center.

The one thing I had going for me that night at Rockefeller University was that I was completely out of my element. I could come in on an angle they might not have thought of.

Here's what I think we have to do to get past our blind date with science: I think we have to go through the three stages of love.
People have been trying to map the stages of love for two or three thousand years now. Some people claim there are eight stages of love; some say six. I'll say there are three because three is easier to remember. Here's what I think they are:
The first stage of love is lust. That's certainly easy to remember.
The second stage is infatuation.
And the third is commitment.
The feeling of lust is what takes place during the blind date, if the date is at all successful.
It's simple, reptile-brain, animal attraction. It's our genes telling us they want to live forever. I may be stretching it

a little, but when we first hear some news about science, I think we have a similar reaction: Our eyes dilating with pleasure, our pulse quickening, we sense that someone has something to tell us that could make us a little smarter or give us some little edge for survival. We listen for an extra second, our eyes locked on the source of our bounty. Just as with the object of our lust, our genes are telling us they want to live forever and this is just another way to do it.

But for this kind of attraction to take place between humans on a blind date— and, by analogy, between the public and science—there's an interesting dynamic that has to take place. Researchers have found that this attraction can happen in the first couple of minutes of an encounter, and it's not so much what's said as the way we present ourselves. Body language and tone of voice account for ninety-three percent of the attraction. What's actually said, only seven percent.

This is something I began to understand when I started interviewing scientists on Scientific American Frontiers. During the eleven years I did the show, I spoke with hundreds of scientists. What I found was that their work became clear–and interesting to a lay audience— to the extent that I could help keep them from sliding into lecture mode. I remember an interview with a scientist in Boston who was an engaging person and whose work was fascinating. I was very curious about it, and I kept asking questions, which she would begin answering in a conversational way and then, I guess realizing that this was part of her regular line of talk, she would slowly turn away from me, face the camera, and go into deep lecture mode. Her voice changed, her face changed—her vocabulary changed. She became almost instantaneously unintelligible. I would tempt her back to me with a passionate display of curiosity. And as soon as she turned toward me, her entire affect became human and warm again. This happened two or three times during our talk, and each time the difference was startling.

This was one of the main reasons the show was successful: We allowed scientists to speak in their own voices. They had the texture and temperature of humanity. They didn't sound like gods from Olympus. They sounded like very, very smart humans.

I think human warmth is vital in establishing instantaneous attraction. But that's just the first stage of love.

To get beyond lust, which tends to be a passing interest, we have to move to the next stage: infatuation.

Here's where emotion comes in. If people are going to remember what they hear, they'll need to have their emotions touched. Research has shown that emotion is what makes us remember, and I think it helps us pay attention, too.

If we tell it right, the story of science can not only arouse our emotions, it can be a great detective story. It's fascinating to hear about a breakthrough as a mystery getting solved. Too often, I think, we hear about the results of the search, without the drama of the search itself. Please don't leave out your mistakes. That's the most dramatic part of the story. Invite us to solve the puzzle along with you, with all its emotional ups and downs.

And give us context. Tell us why this
breakthrough needed to take place. What
was tried by others? Why did it fail? What
did you try along the way? How did you
fail, and how did you succeed? Don't leave
out the blind alleys and the mistakes.
They're fascinating to us. They make
what you do a human enterprise.

But then I thought of my professor a half
century ago in the well of that amphitheater, trying as hard as he could to drill the hard stuff of
science into our heads. Maybe I was asking too
much of him to think he could make chemical
bonds and valences as emotional as the chemistry of Bogart and Bergman in **Casablanca.**

Science is hard to understand and, clearly,
it can't all be absorbed through interesting
stories.
　　There are technical terms that have
to be understood, and they have to be
introduced with a sensitivity to the mind
that's trying to grasp them. When I was a
boy, about nine, I sat and looked at a flame
for an hour. I wondered what it was. It was

too hot to touch, but even if you could, it had no body to it, no weight. I asked my teacher, and she said, "It's oxidation." Ah, I said. Oxidation. I didn't want to offend her, but I thought this was the dumbest thing I'd ever heard. I didn't need another name for it; I needed to know what it was. I needed to hear in the simplest terms what was going on at the end of the candle. I needed her to understand where I was in my mind.

This brings us to the third stage of love: commitment. I'd say that the heart of commitment is finding actual value in the other person. Not the simple attraction of lust or casual interest; not the head-turning fantasies of infatuation—but, rather, both of you finding a real and deep value in the other. This is probably the only stage of love where you actually have to listen to the other person. And because of that, it's when you understand what's going on in that person's mind.

I think the listener can grasp the tough part of science critically and intelligently if it's presented in a way that's both personal and accurate. I think this is possible, as long as we remember that dumbing down is not the goal; clarity is the goal.

Da Vinci said, "Simplicity is the ultimate form of sophistication." But, of course, we should make sure we're not painting a false picture through oversimplification. Einstein said it very well: "Make everything as simple as possible, but no simpler."

On the other hand, Big Al—as one astronomer I interviewed called Einstein— Big Al shouldn't get a totally free pass in the metaphor department. Once reporters were hounding him for a simple explanation of relativity, and finally, in exasperation, he gave a statement to his secretary to pass on to them. He said:

"An hour sitting with a pretty girl on a park bench passes like a minute, but a minute sitting on a hot stove seems like an hour."

That certainly has simplicity going for it—and I guess it's true, as far as it goes— but I have this funny feeling that's not the kind of insight they gave him the Nobel Prize for.

So, if the Great One could get

frustrated occasionally, and oversimplify, the rest of us will certainly not find it easy. There are some real problems in making science clear. For instance, I do believe that the more personal it is, the more vivid it will be . . . and the more it's expressed in the scientist's own voice, the better. But to some extent, this goes against the very nature of science: There's common agreement that the cult of personality should not outweigh the evidence. I think this is one reason that some scientists tend to regard as slightly less scientific those colleagues who achieve great popular fame.

But I believe that in presenting science, if you can bring about a balance of personal energy and scientific rigor, you can accomplish several things at once: You can make the work of the scientist more accessible, and you can help science itself to be seen as the exciting, fun, human thing it is. Any bright kid can see it as something he or she could pursue. You can even introduce a whole new way of thinking to many people—one based on evidence rather than opinion or magic.

But to do this, we have to be aware of what's going on in the listener's head.

I'm sure this is what every good teacher does. I do something like this in my work, too. Probably all of us who put ourselves in front of an audience have to learn to be aware of what's going on in the mind of the listener. When I write, when I act, or when I just tell a funny story, I'm constantly working on setting up expectations in the mind of the audience. And then messing up those expectations, and eventually resolving them in a pleasurable way.

It's like the older couple who went to court to get a divorce. And the judge just couldn't understand why they were divorcing. He said to the man, "You're ninety-eight years old, your wife is ninety-six. You've been married for seventy years. Why would you want to get a divorce now?" And the man said, "We've been waiting for the children to die."

If you track what you're thinking, when you hear that trivial little story, it has almost the same structure as Oedipus Rex.

It does.

Someone is trying to figure something

out. Why do you want a divorce? This
doesn't make sense. We identify with
the task. Look at the length of time you
waited. We agree. We press for an answer
with the judge. Then the husband gives
the answer, and the result is both inevitable
and surprising. As soon as he says it, you
track back and you realize that the length
of time they were married was the deciding
factor. During such a long marriage, things
happen, conversations take place, decisions
are made that wouldn't have taken place in
a marriage of normal length. You've been
led down a path that quickly, surprisingly,
doubles back on itself. An expectation has
been set up in your mind; then it's been
played with, and then resolved, in an
unexpected way.

In Oedipus Rex, the city is cursed, and
Oedipus has to find who's responsible.
Years earlier, he had a standoff on a narrow
road with a man going the opposite way
and, rashly, killed him. As it turns out, the
man was his own father. The surprise is
that Oedipus himself is the culprit he's
been searching for. With the elderly couple,
the surprise is that they've been waiting for

the kids to die. One's tragic and the other is funny, but I think most good stories contain this play on expectations.

This kind of thing doesn't come naturally to everyone, but it can be taught systematically.

The word systematic is terrifically important in all of this. Good communication can be taught. But for it to have a lasting effect—for it to become a part of someone's core—I think it has to be taught systematically, and over time.

Here's the model. In my field, a hundred years ago in Russia, Konstantin Stanislavsky showed that the art of acting could be taught systematically. He called it the System, and it was later renamed the Method in the American version. Until then, acting was a mysterious process in which only a talented few could shine. He didn't make every student a genius, but he found he could elevate many to a higher standard of ability. It wasn't that ordinary people selected at random became geniuses. But what did happen was that even minimally talented people could become proficient. The level of everyone rose significantly. Geniuses still stood out. But through study, you could become competent. I think this model can be used to inspire a course of study in communication for scientists. But it has to take place over time; it can't be a crash course of a few hours or a few weeks.

What I would love to see is scientists learning the skills of communication throughout their science education; and all forms of communication–written and verbal. But I'm not talking about a crash course in speaking in sound bites. I'm talking about developing scientists' ability to speak accurately about their work, but in a personal, vivid way that makes the listeners' brains light up with pleasure and excitement.

I realize that science is an endlessly vast and difficult set of subjects to teach, and I'm sure there's hardly time in the curriculum now to get in all the science students need. So how can you squeeze in communication? That's an important objection. But look at the inefficiencies in the system we have now. How much better and faster would things go if undergraduates were being taught by graduate students who had been trained, themselves, in the skills of communication?

The problem now is that only people who are naturally talented with words rise to the top as communicators. We've accepted a system in which scientists are trained rigorously in science, but the communication of science has been left completely to chance.

And it's not just ability with words that will make science vivid to us. It's the ability to let the person you are inside you, the authentic you, come out: to be able to express not just what you know, but who you are. This doesn't have to diminish the hard science, but it can go a long way toward making the science clear and available.

When I talked to the graduating class at Caltech, I asked them to devote a significant part of their lives to figuring out how to share their love of science with the rest of us. And I'm asking the scientists here tonight the same thing.

Be personal about science; arouse our

lust for it. Tell us a story and make our hearts quicken.

Let's listen to one another, let's commit to one another.

Let's fall in love.

After the talk, as we walked to the president's house for dinner, Paul Nurse told me he had been interested for some time in this problem. He said that for several years in England, he had run training programs to help scientists improve their communication skills, and in one he had even brought in actors to work with them. I knew Paul was naturally talented at holding an audience, but I could see now that he had been methodical about it, too. He had worked at it systematically, the way he had worked at science.

Fifty years earlier, I had thought I couldn't stay in that dim amphitheater if I wanted to be an actor. But Paul had brought actors **into** the amphitheater. He was reconnecting the cord between the hemispheres. He was pulling the continents back together.

It was a while before I began to see what I was telling myself in this talk: to listen. I was asking scientists to listen to what their audience was thinking, but really I was telling **myself** to listen, too. To not think that my present interests defined all there was to me. To move outside myself to what was in the other person's mind, no matter how alien it seemed. To find what was interesting and valuable in their strangeness.

I could see now that my father wasn't asking me to follow his dream, but to find my own and not limit myself only to what interested me then.

Pushing past our fathers, like Oedipus on the narrow road, is one of the ways we move on into adulthood, and I had pushed mine aside. I had undervalued him. I had thought of my father as a vain actor with few interests. But, in fact, he was curious and, in a way, even studious. He was excited by the land when we moved to the country, and he sent away for pamphlets from the Department of Agriculture. He studied them at night and transplanted olive trees by day. He had gone to Stuyvesant High School in Manhattan, where you had to be good at math just to get in. He told me often that his favorite book was about the scientists who had discovered microbes. He did have interests outside himself, but I didn't listen for them. He might have been vain, but he was far less of a show-off about his curiosity than I was about mine, and I mistook that for a lack of interest. I mistook his gentleness for passivity. How could he urge me to find my own way if he insisted on the road I take? He gave me the freedom to discover it for myself. It was the way he taught me to act in the burlesque sketches we did together: "Say that line a few times. As many as you feel is good. Usually three is good, but whatever you feel." And it was the way he pointed me toward the chemistry class. "Just give it a try," he said.

In gently urging me to explore, he gave meaning to my life that I think neither of us expected. I might not have responded at that very moment, but eventually I did, and it gave me the nerve to go places that scare me, but where I find excitement and adventure. I've wound up going where he wanted me to go: toward all the things that could interest me, if I'd let them.

Long after we had gone our separate ways, I met my father on the road again—and this time I let him pass.

Chapter 15

Celebrity and Its Discontents

While I was playing on television in M*A*S*H, a poll was taken of schoolchildren, and the appalling finding was that my face was more recognizable to them than Abraham Lincoln's. Lincoln: the man who freed the slaves, who wrote the Gettysburg Address, whose face is on the penny; if only he could have appeared weekly in prime time, he could have been somebody.

A delegation from the magazine that did the poll came to the set and took my picture, and we had lunch under a tent in the Malibu mountains where we shot the exteriors. There was a lot of laughing and joking. They were delighted to be on the set of a popular show, and I think they expected me to be delighted by how well known my face was. I was amazed, but I was a little uneasy, too. That afternoon captured what all of us feel about celebrity. We don't understand it. We chuckle at it, even as it touches us in countless ways. But what exactly **is** it? Three decades later, I was thinking about it again in the middle of the night.

I couldn't sleep. I got up three times during the night to sit at the computer and fix a word or straighten a twisted metaphor. The next day, I would be giving one of those talks that I had no business delivering. My friend Mike, the psychoanalyst, had asked if I'd give a talk at his hospital. At first I'd said no, and then I thought maybe I did have something to talk about. I had been thinking for a while that one of the ways people have of looking for meaning in their lives is celebrity. It's one of the ways we hope to live forever. Maybe by talking with Mike's group about this, I could understand it better. I said yes.

Amazingly, I had agreed to give the Grand Rounds lecture at the Weill Cornell Medical College of Cornell University. The audacity of this didn't really hit me until the night before the talk.

Why had I thought I could say anything to a hundred psychiatrists that they would find remotely interesting? How could their response be anything but one that ranged from condescension to outrage? I had to stop this thing of testing myself all the time. It was getting ridiculous. There was enough adrenaline in my bloodstream to get a herd of cattle across a river. I took a pill and drifted off.

When morning came, I went into performance mode. **I've done this before, and I can do it again,** I thought. But a voice in my head was saying, **Excuse me? You keep doing things you have** never **done before and shouldn't even consider doing.**

In the cab on the way to the hospital, I tried to read through my talk while the driver raced through traffic with his radio at full volume. He was listening to a program in Russian, which I couldn't understand, but still, it distracted me. And then it got worse. He got on his cell phone and started screaming at someone in passionate Russian. This was followed by the guy on the radio talking even louder. Distracted, the driver took a wrong turn, and I was afraid I'd be late for my talk. I raised my voice above all the Russian coming from the front seat.

"Can we go north instead of south? And can you please get off the phone? In the first place, it's against the law, and in the second place, it's making me late."

"I **have** to be on phone. This man is making me crazy. Is not patriotic what he says. I am American. I am proud to be."

"Yes, good, but can you put the phone away and drive?"

"I can't put phone away. I am on radio."

He was on the phone with a call-in radio show. I was going to be late for a talk on celebrity because the cabdriver was in the middle of his fifteen minutes. He made a U-turn, and driving as fast as he could with one hand, while screaming in Russian, he got me to the lecture hall on time and on edge. It was the perfect preparation for the confusion I felt about the subject I was there to talk about.

Thank you for taking the time to see me. I'll get right into it. Here are my symptoms:

I see strangers staring at me in the street. When I pass a group of people, I hear them saying my name behind my back. People I'm sure I don't know try to

touch me. Some of them try to kiss me. Once I hired a guard because I believed a woman was coming after me with a handgun. And sometimes I'm asked to speak in front of learned people about subjects in which I have no training—and I do it.

Actually, I know what I'm experiencing. It's called celebrity and its discontents.

Celebrity, of course, seems trivial—the insignificant pairing of underdeveloped rock groupies with borderline narcissists, preening across the footlights—but actually, it's all around us. The drive over with the cabbie was a small example of how the public and the private are blurred now. And the impact celebrity has on us isn't confined to shallow entertainment. It influences almost everything we do. It's been doing it for centuries.

The Greeks saw fame in two ways: as the reward for a virtuous life, but also as rumor and scandal.

Homer wrote about honor and renown: the public recognition that came to a person who lived life in the fullest flower of self-worth. But on the other hand, Hesiod, who lived around the same time as Homer, said: "Do as I tell you and keep away from the gossip of people. For Pheme (which was a name for both fame and rumor) is an evil thing, by nature. She's a light weight to lift up, oh very easy, but heavy to carry, and hard to put down again. Pheme never disappears entirely once many people have talked her big. In fact, she really is some sort of goddess." This was the dark side of fame: fame as a goddess of rumor, gossip, and report.

So as long as 2,700 years ago, people saw that fame had two sides to it. But in our world, even the renown that comes as a reward for virtue can be burned around the edges by the goddess of rumor. They said then that Rumor flew with the speed of a raging fire, but now, with modern communication, she flies at the speed of light.

If you go to Google, you can see a fascinating example of the influence that the goddess of rumor has on our lives. Google began a new service a few months ago called Google Trends. You can chart the popularity of various search terms around the world. I thought it would be interesting to compare the number of searches for Angelina to the number for Katrina. Hurricane Katrina hit in late August 2005. It was one of the deadliest hurricanes in the history of the United States, taking at least 1,800 lives. In September, Katrina far outshone any interest the public had in the actress Angelina Jolie. By October, though, their chart lines were crisscrossing each other. In December, Angelina broke through and pretty much stayed above Katrina. The week it was announced that she and Brad Pitt were having a baby, the search term Angelina Jolie got more attention than the term Iraq. And it stayed that way for months. According to Google, the news media during this period were consistently covering Katrina and the Iraq war far more than they were covering these two actors, but that's not what people were searching for on Google.

Celebrity gets into the most serious parts of our lives. There was a time when politicians simply **courted** celebrities. Now they try to become celebrities themselves.

> Simple name recognition is one of the benchmarks of success in politics. Candidates spend millions trying to get it. Name recognition is so powerful that every few years an election is won by someone whose name is well known but who, at the time, is actually dead—which isn't all that bad, because the dead ones do less damage than the live ones.

I found out how much stock politicians put in fame a few years after M*A*S*H hit and I had been placed up on the pantheon of recognizable faces. A delegation from a political club in New Jersey flew out to the set and asked me to run for the U.S. Senate. I found it hard to believe they were serious. "No, no," they said. "We mean it. We want to back you." I thanked them but said I didn't want to be a politician; I wanted to act and write. And that's all I was qualified to do. Their answer was, "But you could **win**."

Eventually they left, disappointed.

It's not just politics, of course. Celebrity is tied to the way we sell things to one another.

Twenty percent of all the ads in the United States use celebrities—twice as many as ten years ago. And public health is tied to celebrity, both for good and for bad.

The good influence has been called the Couric effect because when Katie Couric broadcast her colonoscopy on network television, the rate of colonoscopies in the country went up more than 20 percent over the next nine months. Before that, screening rates rose after Ronald Reagan's colon cancer and Magic Johnson's infection with HIV.

But celebrity also affects public health negatively. There's the phenomenon of suicide copycats, which, it's said, are more likely to occur when a celebrity commits suicide. And countless young girls become bulimic to be like famous models.

I was hitting them with all these figures because I wanted to make sure they didn't regard this as a completely frivolous topic. But I wanted to get under the numbers somehow and try to understand this strange part of all our lives. I've actually lived this phenomenon, and for me it's not so much a question of how big it is as how deep it goes—and how utterly mysterious it is.

CELEBRITY AND ITS DISCONTENTS

For most of my life, between my father's celebrity and my own, I've been able to observe what happens to people on both sides of the line separating celebrities from the rest of the world. My first exposure to fame was on Hollywood Boulevard when I was eight years old, and I didn't like it. It was about midnight. We'd just seen a movie. I was walking with my parents, and a girl about sixteen came up behind us. She punched my father in the back and screamed, "You son of a bitch!" and then she ran off down the street. My parents saw that I was shaken by this, and they tried to help me understand it. They explained that some people don't know how to react to people they've seen on the screen and that I shouldn't let it make me afraid. But it seemed to me that being afraid of a person like that was a good idea.

A few months later, I had my next look at fame—with Bogart. My father was shooting a movie at Warner Brothers, and he had asked someone in the publicity department to show me around the back lot. We were walking down one of the old New York streets, with its fake brownstone apartment buildings and the facades of theaters and banks. Suddenly he stopped in his tracks and looked at a small man who was sitting in a director's chair, in the middle of a conversation.

"That's Humphrey Bogart," he said. "Ask him for his autograph."

He handed me a scrap of paper, but I didn't know what I was supposed to do with it. I had never been part of this ritual before. He gave me a little push toward Bogart, and I walked over and held out the paper. Bogart took it, scribbled on it, and handed it back without looking at me. "Here, kid," he said in that voice. I looked at the paper with an illegible scrawl on it. Why had I been sent over to interrupt him for **this?** I kept the autograph on the dresser in my bedroom for months, and every day I would look at it—not to remind myself I had met a famous person, but to wonder why anyone would think this little scrap of paper was valuable.

I asked myself that question again twenty-five years later when suddenly people were coming up to me with little pieces of paper in their hands. The success of **M*A*S*H** was so great that at first I was stunned by the attention that came to me. I had to figure out a strategy or I wouldn't be able to move down a crowded street without signing my name every few feet. After a while, I started offering to shake hands instead. It seemed more personal. It wouldn't result in that cold scribble of Bogart's that sat on the dresser. I knew my life had changed one day when I was sitting in a seat on the aisle, waiting for a Broadway play to start. Someone came over with a piece of paper. Then someone else, and then another. Within a few minutes, there was a line of people stretching up the aisle to the back of the theater. I was signing fast, trying to be accommodating but wishing the lights would dim so everyone would go back to their seats and I could go back to being a member of the audience. Curtains seldom go up later than six or seven minutes past the hour, but it was getting to be twelve, then fifteen minutes past curtain time.

Finally, an usher came over to me apologetically. "Do you mind if we start the play now?" she said.

"God, yes. Please. You're waiting for **me**? I'm waiting for you."

I'd been thinking the stage manager would start the play on time, but now I couldn't rely on people to behave in expected ways. Having stepped into this sticky tar pit of celebrity, I now trailed a mysterious aroma that had a peculiar effect on people.

People occasionally think there's something magical about celebrities. There were the letters from people on the verge of suicide. Only I could help them. And sometimes people act as if fame has made you immune to ordinary catastrophes: On **Scientific American Frontiers,** we did a story on the Leaning Tower of Pisa. As we walked inside the tower, the custodian was telling me that it was still tipping over a little more every year, and unless they could fix it, it wouldn't just tip over, the pressure on the middle of the structure would make it explode. We passed a sign that read "No one permitted beyond this point." I asked if people were allowed to climb the tower.

"Oh no," he said, "not anymore. But in your case, we made an exception."

Once, in a torrential rain, a cop was turning people away from a bridge that was about to be swept down the river, but when he saw my face, he waved me through. Fortunately, I didn't go.

Interestingly, people often lose motor control. A few weeks after my face was newly famous, I was walking toward a couple coming out of an ice-cream shop. The man was carrying an ice-cream cone, and when he saw me, the cone flew into the air, looped around, and hit the pavement ice cream first. His wife had no idea what had come over him. "Harry. I don't believe you."

More than motor control, they lose control of

syntax. It's very common for someone to come up to a famous person and say, "You're my biggest fan." This has happened not just a few times to **me,** but many times to every well-known person I've asked about it. "You're my biggest fan," they say.

I wondered what the psychiatrists would make of this.

What does this mean? They're starting to say, "You're my favorite . . ." and midway confusing it with "I'm your fan." There seems to be a confusion of identity. I am you and you are me. It sounds a little like what Freud said in Civilization and Its Discontents: **"At the height of being in love the boundary between ego and object threatens to melt away. Against all the evidence of his senses, a man who is in love declares that 'I' and 'you' are one. . . ."**

Why these exact words, over and over again? "You're my biggest fan." Is there an unconscious desire to resist the power they feel the famous person has over them? You're my fan. You don't have power over me, I have power over you. Or maybe not. Maybe in this case a cigar is just a cigar.

Sometimes, although rarely, there is actual hostility. I was scouting locations for **Sweet Liberty,** a movie I was going to direct on Long Island. It had been a long fourteen-hour day when I stopped to fill up at a gas station late at night. A short, wiry man came over to the car and leaned in the window. He asked for an autograph. I said I was sorry, I didn't give autographs, but I'd be glad to shake his hand. He said, "I don't want to shake your hand! You know something? You're not that great an actor. You just play the same part over and over." He was giving me a critical review at midnight next to a gas pump. Then he got more specific. He called to a friend: "Let's beat this guy up." His fantasy disappointed and his rage aroused, he was no longer the pleasant Dr. Jekyll I had offered to shake hands with. I pulled my face back from the open window and drove off on an empty tank.

But it usually isn't hostility that surfaces. People's emotions are stirred in a way I don't fully understand. I was having dinner in a restaurant once, and a few tables away a woman in her thirties put down her fork and stared at me with a vulnerable, confused expression. It was early in my career, and I didn't know how to react. Should I nod? Should I say something? I decided to do nothing and went on eating. A few seconds later, there were tears coming down her face. I didn't know what to do. I froze. We sat there, staring at each other. And then she started sobbing. Big, heaving sobs. She got up from the table, her dinner half-eaten, and left the restaurant.

Why are we so disoriented by the sight of a famous person? We've seen these famous people on a screen in a darkened room, which is a dreamlike state. Is that why, when that person steps magically out of our dreams and into reality, we become disoriented?

Sometimes we think that objects touched by the famous have some special importance. My family and I were having breakfast in a pancake house once, and as we were leaving, the family at the next table asked my wife, "Is he finished with his napkin?" It was sticky from syrup and egg stains, but they took it as a souvenir. To some extent, **most** of us can behave this way. I certainly have. I bought an original Rembrandt etching once because it was beautiful—and also, when I think about it, because Rembrandt had touched it. Later, I was afraid I might have bought a fake, but I never quite found out for sure. (This way, he **might** have touched it.)

Fame is an aphrodisiac. It bestows sex appeal

on you. When Bill Clinton was running for president, he appeared on MTV and a young woman in the audience asked him if he wore boxers or briefs. Soon after I started on M*A*S*H, I was asked the same question by two young women who came over to me in a bar. They said they couldn't get over having laughed at all the funny things I said on television. Hoping to defuse their interest, I introduced them to the two good-looking young writers from the show I was there with. These were the people who had actually **written** the funny things I said. But they weren't famous, and the women had no interest in them **or** in their underwear.

We tend to think that **rich** and **famous** go together, but fame takes more getting used to than being rich does. The difficult part of celebrity is when you're recognized not for what you do, but simply for being famous. It can be moving when someone tells you that your work has affected them in some way. But when you're only a facade, as recognizable as the Empire State Building and about as emotionally moving, the feeling is different. I had known, of course, that signing on for a television show would involve getting better known, and I thought I could handle it—

but now, people were pulling at me, yanking at my clothing, grabbing me.

I felt I was being hunted. For months, I had night terrors in which I saw a shadowy figure in my bedroom in the middle of the night, glaring at me, and I would wake up screaming. After a while, I would wake up while he was strangling me. This was a little harder to take than the checks that were accumulating in the dresser drawer.

After the shadowy figure stopped dropping in every night, I got a visit on the set one day from the FBI. Two agents came to tell me a young woman had escaped from a mental hospital in Florida. She had a gun and was headed for California, where she was going to get revenge on Alan Alda and Clint Eastwood. It seems Clint and I had abducted her in Los Angeles a couple of years earlier, and she was coming after me with a handgun. I thanked the agents, and we put a guard on the door at Stage Nine for a while.

More difficult, though, than the way people react to who they **think** you are is that you can't be who you really are. Albert Camus felt that the public man can't be private in public or he destroys the public image.

Something like this happened to the soccer

player Zinedine Zidane (known affectionately in France as Zizou) in 2006 during the World Cup. He was thrown out of the game when he head-butted another player. Zidane, who later said that his mother and sister had been insulted repeatedly by the player, acted in a moment of rashness, not as a famous athlete with constraints, but as the private person he was underneath. A lot of articles were published about this, with some writers picking up on the Camus idea, suggesting that Zidane, consciously or unconsciously, was lashing out not only at the player who had insulted him, but also, as one said, at "the unlivable role he had been slotted into by the French." He had to play the part of Zizou, an idealized national hero—a role that was impossible to live up to. In this way, the public image can be a cage. It can inhibit growth or change of any kind. Popular artists have trouble deepening the work they got popular for, and politicians have trouble simply changing their minds.

As your public persona grows, it becomes based, in part, on some aspect of you, but to a large extent on descriptions of you by people who don't actually know you. The image flies around like the goddess of

rumor and builds until it may be seriously
at odds with who you really are. In any
case, it's not a three-dimensional picture. If
you have any desire at all to be human, you
want to have at least one more dimension
beyond the two that are allotted to a
cartoon character. But it's hard to escape
the public character you become. Mine was
"Mr. Nice Guy." It became my nickname.
It started early in the run of M*A*S*H
with a Newsweek headline: "Nice Guy
Finishes First." The headline hooked into a
cliché and turned it around slightly, lodging
in the minds of other writers, who repeated
it, amplifying the effect. I didn't mind it
at first, but when I began to see it was
becoming my identity, I bristled. Especially
when I started being told I was "too nice."
It became harder to campaign for the Equal
Rights Amendment and legal equality
when people could dismiss my arguments
as the sentimental oozings of a weakling.
But once the phrase caught on, it was
unstoppable. Ten years later, the writer of
the article introduced himself to me. "Hi,"
he said apologetically, "I'm the one who
started it." But to be admired and derided

311

at the same time was probably going to happen anyway, and according to Samuel Johnson, I should have welcomed it. He said, "It is advantageous to an author, that his book should be attacked as well as praised. Fame is a shuttlecock. If it be struck only at one end of the room, it will soon fall to the ground. To keep it up, it must be struck at both ends." But that sounds to me more like a description of why fame isn't worth it.

I was able to wait it out, and eventually it pretty much went away. Camus, who died young, never really had the time to wait it out. In an interview he gave when he was forty-five, the year before he died, a reporter asked him: "Do you find yourself at ease in your personality as a writer?" He said, "Very much at ease in my private relationships. But the public aspect of my calling, which I have never liked, is becoming unbearable."

But none of us is immune; people keep coming along who are sure that fame will solve their problems. Instead, I've seen them become despondent. It turned out they had the same problems as before, but magnified, and now they even had a few more. We suppose that the attention we'll get will feel like we're being adored. It never occurs to us that it might feel, instead, like being hunted. Sometimes it's both.

As loved as she was, Princess Diana was also hunted. Her public persona was loved by a whole nation who never knew her. They loved her so much that after she died and Elizabeth didn't quickly make a public display of grieving, they began to reconsider their love for a queen they had loved and whom they had also never known.

I met Diana a few years before she died. I met her because I was famous and she was famous. I was acting in a play in the West End of London, and one day, for some reason I can't remember, all the theater people in town were invited to lunch. I went and was surprised to see that I was seated next to Princess Diana. I knew by now that the only way to speak to a famous person was as a person, not as someone famous; to talk about their job, their interests, something simple and human. When famous people meet, they often go out of their way to speak simply, idiomatically, sometimes even using slang and coarse language to deflect any sense of trying to appear special to the other person. When I see photographs of world figures with their heads thrown back in abandoned laughter, I think one of them has probably just said something startlingly ordinary to break the ice.

I tried to be direct with Diana, but it came out a little forced.

"It must be hard, having to go out day after day and make these public appearances. Probably at a lot of places where you don't even really want to go." If I was awkward, she was gracious and answered me simply and with a certain amount of force.

"It was **very** hard in the beginning. And they didn't give me any help at all—the family. They just shoved me out there and let me figure it out for myself."

She was angry, and I was surprised at her candor, because she was still a member of the British royal family at that point. We chatted some more, and the lunch was over, but I remembered her vulnerability.

Then six years later, pursued by paparazzi in a Paris tunnel, her car crashed and a few hours later she died. People around the world were sorrowful. And I found myself angry at the photographers who I felt had hounded her to her death. Three days later, I had to fly to California, and as I got off the plane, there was a photographer waiting in the terminal. I hadn't been on prime-time television for years. I wasn't hot. There was no reason to be lying in wait for me. But these guys would bribe people working for the airlines for a look at the manifest list and then take pictures of anyone well known, in the hope they might do something inappropriate, or be with someone they shouldn't, or stagger off the plane drunk. I ignored him, but then he began that ritualistic backward walk: always facing me, snapping the shutter, and flashing his strobe in my face; leading me in a compliant dance of self-betrayal. Hiding my face from him would be as good a picture as posing and smiling; even better. I had a flash of anger. I turned on him and put my face in his. He took a step back toward the wall.

"How dare you?" I said. "How dare you do this, three days after what just happened?" I felt she had been hunted, as I had been when fame first hit me. But I had had the time and the luck to adjust. For me, the discontents of celebrity had leveled off, but hers had only deepened.

The photographer didn't know what I was talking about. I was blaming him for being a member of the tribe that had killed her, and he looked at me as if I were a little out of my head. And to some extent, I was. A touch more testosterone and I might have turned into Zidane. But my anger didn't change anything. It contributed nothing to my contentedness.

> For this discontent to go away, or at least diminish, I think the trick is to somehow be able to live both a public life and a private life at the same time, without one threatening or destroying the value of the other.

I looked at my watch.

> I see we're coming to the end of the hour— and it's time for the cure. If you don't mind, I'll go ahead and administer it myself.
> I don't know about anyone else, but for me, the antidote to the discontents of the public face is to be as authentic as possible—to be simply who I am, both in my public face and in my private one.
> So what we'll do is, we'll take this boy—born into a life of illusion, bred by a mother who had hallucinations, trained in the art of being someone else, and who found himself known for someone he only

partly resembled—and we'll give him a new identity.

After a life of trying many others, this one may work best. The identity we'll give him is himself.

I felt pretty good about the talk. I had tried to be honest with them, and putting my tangled feelings into words had unraveled a few knots in them. Their questions were generous and supportive. I'd spoken in a place where I didn't really belong, and I seemed to have got away with it again.

A few weeks later, I was having dinner with Mona Ackerman, a therapist friend who had been there that day. She had listened closely, and she'd saved her question for when we were at dinner. "You told us in your talk," she said, "that you never wanted to be famous. I wondered about that."

"I didn't. I never wanted to be famous."

"Really? Not at all?"

It was an innocent question that made my eyes lock on hers. How honest had I been with myself?

"Well, I guess it's possible . . . maybe I wanted it a little."

"Why did you choose show business, I wonder?"

"Yes, well, that's true. . . ."

We looked at each other for a few seconds—and smiled. She had me. Of course I'd wanted it. It was a way to live forever. There was even a moment in my life when I'd worked out my strategy for eternal life. Sitting there with Mona, I flashed on it.

I was in my twenties, in a Howard Johnson's near Times Square with a couple of other actors. We were passing time between auditions, and I mentioned that I was teaching myself to write and that I wanted to write really well because otherwise my work wouldn't last very long. Writing lasted, I said, but stage work evaporated as it was being performed.

I smile now at the young man I was then. I assumed that whatever I wrote would be taken to heart by millions, and through my work I'd go on living. I didn't know what the years in between have taught me: It **all** evaporates. When film was invented, they thought it would allow stage performances to last forever; but silver nitrate burned like flash paper, and celluloid turned to dust. One day colors burst on the screen, and the next day they faded. Brilliant hues turned to green and eventually to pink ghosts. Everything goes. Chaucer needs to be translated now. In time, so will Shakespeare. And just as books rot and go to worm, and Edison cylinders gave way to wax and wax to vinyl—everything we do, or make, or think of, will give way to something else.

Celebrity won't let us live forever. It barely lets us live for now. So I think I'll cross that off the list. But what's left? Isn't there **anything** that can give us that jolt we're looking for—that feeling of satisfaction that lets us know how good it is that we're here? Maybe there's one. But it's so ordinary, so foolishly simple, it's easy to miss. I've walked right by it time after time.

Chapter 16

Bosco's Belly

We were just finishing a comforting bottle of Brunello when my friend Arnold looked across the table and put down his glass. He'd been listening to my ruminations with compassion. **Where was I going with this?** I wondered. **Was I asking questions that had answers?**

"You know what you should do? This will tell you how you really feel about all this. You should write one more talk. But a special one."

"Like what?"

"If you were asked to give a commencement talk on your deathbed, what would you say?"

Arnold Steinhardt is a great violinist who is also a shockingly good writer. He can draw sense out of the simplest words the way he can draw music out of catgut and horsehair. So I paid attention. What **would** I tell the kids if I were writing a commencement talk on my deathbed? Would it bring me closer to the heart of it?

I doubt that on my actual deathbed I'll use my time trying to crank out a few fresh platitudes, but I thought I'd see what I could come up with as if it were my last chance to make sense of it all.

So here goes. Today, for all you graduates who are moving out into the world, looking with hope toward the future, my message is this: "Go forth. And stay there."

What do I mean by this? Do I mean you should get out of town? Go away and not come back? Well, in a way, yes. I'm saying, Go; set off on an adventure like Lewis and Clark's—but don't come back to where you started. Lewis and Clark almost died on their adventure, but they had a worse time when they came back. Instead, why not keep exploring, keep learning? Why fall back into old ways? Why ever give up trying to get where you've never been before? Someplace that, maybe, no one has **ever** been? Take what you need to survive in the wild, and go. When you get there, take what you find and make what you need to **keep** going. Go with someone you can lie out under the stars with and who can help you tell the mud from the quicksand as you cut a path through the unknown.

But whatever you do, and this may sound odd on commencement day: Don't go looking for Meaning. I once took that trip myself, thinking it would be fun and easy. I would look back at all the things I've said on days like this—urging young people in one way or another toward a life of meaning—and the answer would be clear. But I've come to hate the word. It's meaningless. My dear friends, are you looking for meaning? Don't do it. I've driven myself crazy with it. I have the distinct suspicion now that there is no hidden meaning to life. Looking for one is just our problem-solving brain chasing its tail—its long, lizardly, snake-brain tail. Whenever I've wanted some meaning, I've had to make it myself. It wasn't included in the box from the store.

Or, as it says on a plaque a friend gave me, "What if the hokey-pokey is really what it's all about?"

Instead of driving yourself crazy, I'd go for something simple:

1. Find someone to laugh with.
2. Find something to laugh at (yourself is always good).
3. Keep moving.

If I've ever had a sense of meaning, it's been in simply experiencing my life: just noticing I was alive. That may be all there is. Marcus Aurelius said that all we have is the present moment. Twenty centuries ago, he understood what brain scientists have lately discovered: that **now** exists for just a brief moment in our brains—maybe five to seven seconds. Everything else is memory or thinking about the future, neither of which ever turns out to be what we think it is. But for me, that brief moment of **now** can be a fizzy quaff on a hot day.

Just noticing life can be the whole bottle of beer. Nature is an intoxicating, tantalizing puzzle, a pyrotechnic display. I tell my grandchildren: "You're **bored?** If you're bored, you're not paying attention." I picked up this pithy saying from an article in a magazine, and I use it all the time on them, but they don't seem to know what I mean by it. They look at me oddly. That's okay. I wouldn't have understood it at their age, either.

The soft belly of Bosco, my grandchildren's

dog; the dreamy look in his eye when you scratch his belly: This is the meaning of life. Both for me and for him.

When my brain gets frisky and I try to think beyond Bosco's belly, it always boils down to the same two questions. One was what my young friend asked over coffee so long ago in a restaurant in Times Square. The restaurant is gone now, but the question lingers: **Why not end it? Is there a point to living?** And I think, **Of course there's a point:** life **is the point.** That's when the ancient Greek looks out at me from the pages of a book and asks: **But what is the** good **life?** The Greek, like the restaurant, is long gone, but the question hangs around.

And **that's** when it really matters what value we place on things. I had a friend who lived the good life. At least it seemed so to him. He wrote books that were read by millions of people, he had houses around the world. And he also liked to spend most of his waking hours in a bottle of gin. So between gin and sleeping, he was unconscious about two-thirds of the time. If I were sentenced by a court to a life like that, I think I would appeal.

Whatever this thing is called—meaning, significance, satisfaction, fulfillment—I've looked for it in art and in love; in learning, friendship, faith, family, and in being helpful; even in pure motion—in just keeping busy. I haven't found that any single one of them does the trick. If I stick with any of them too long, it loses its flavor on the bedpost and I have to switch over to one of the others. I find it for a time; I dig into a meal of it, and before I know it, I'm hungry again.

I do have an embarrassingly big appetite. In my thirties, I hit the jackpot in every way. I had everything: a loving wife, happy children, work I could be proud of, money, friends, even the chance to devote myself a little to the well-being of other people. I was truly happy. And one day I said to myself, **Is this all there is to life—happiness?**

That's more than an appetite. It's piggish. But I was willing to work hard to taste as much as I could of all the things that are supposed to bring the deepest, most lasting satisfaction. And then it turned out that pursuing it doesn't always do it. Sometimes sitting quietly and letting it come to you is what does it. But you never know which it is. Sometimes it's both at once.

Squeezing the most out of life seems to involve some mysterious mix of floating without a care and at the same time working as hard as possible. It's snoozing like a dog in a patch of sun on the living room floor while keeping twelve plates in the air in the kitchen. It's motion and stillness, and both at once. It's being Silent Sam and Scheherazade at the same time.

So it all ends up in some damn Zen paradox. I should have known.

In a way, though, I like all this uncertainty. It makes things more exciting. It ups the ante. Even when I **was** on my deathbed four years ago in a grimy little emergency room in Chile, I thought, **Okay, this may be the end of it; I'd better leave a note for the woman I love.** I didn't pray or hope for an afterlife, or regret the life I'd lived. And I certainly didn't waste time thinking about my so-called accomplishments. I just took care of business. I kind of like looking into the abyss.

But you're graduating today. I don't want to dump too much uncertainty on you right before you go out into a world that's **filled** with randomness. You need confidence.

I'm going to drop the imaginary deathbed talk and switch to one I gave at Southampton College on Long Island in 2003. It's a little bleak here and there, but mostly it's hopeful.

We people in the commencement speech racket have a few standard ways of going about it. Sometimes we ignore the graduates completely and talk right over their heads to the newspapers or to shareholders—or even to other governments, while announcing foreign policy. If it's okay with you, though, I'd like to talk today straight to the graduating class.

Forty-seven years ago, I was sitting out there where you are—well, not exactly where you are—it was on a large lawn in the Bronx. But I was sitting where you are in every other way while some guy, I forget who, was laying out a lot of platitudes for us. He was probably telling us about the word commencement. That's a popular theme. This is graduation day, but it's not the end of something; it's the beginning of something . . . the beginning of the rest of your life. That's a catchy way to start, calling attention to the fact that this event has had the wrong name for maybe six hundred years.

Well, actually, it's the right name, because around the year 1314, commencement meant the initiation of someone into an order, and in a college, it meant taking a full degree. But we know nobody's going to run out and look that up because that's the kind of thing you did during your education—which we know is now over.

He was also probably telling us, "You Are Our Future." Another popular theme. Well, you're not exactly our future. By the time you have any power, we may be outta here. And you're not even your future, because the funny thing about the future is it never gets here.

But it sounds nice to say you're our future. Sort of gives you some status on a big day—a little going-away present.

But this is forty-seven years later. The world is different now, a lot more complex and potentially more lethal. Little pleasantries are not going to do the job today.

There's an old curse that goes like this: May you have the misfortune to live in interesting times. We have the miserable luck to live in fascinating times. As a species we know so much, and as a nation we're so powerful, that it sometimes seems

to me our future may be like a pencil
balancing on its point. Any little thing
could tip it, and depending on which way
the pencil falls, we could either enter a
golden age or see the birth of a darker dark
age than we've ever seen before.

But it probably just seems that way.
Probably we'll muddle on—continuing to
avoid both utopia and apocalypse. Which
will be good, because all the utopias we've
tried so far have been pipe dreams. And as
for apocalypse, we have a knack for saying,
"Not apocalypse now. Apocalypse later,"
and getting away with it.

So I guess that's the daunting task
ahead of you: bravely muddling on.

And I'm here to tell you how to do it.
I'm your man. Of all the people they could
have picked to send you on your way with
a final word of wisdom, they picked me.
You are so lucky. I'm the perfect one to
talk to you—because I learned practically
nothing in college. Well, I learned a couple
of things, and I'm sure you learned even
more. But believe me, you have yet to learn
the thing that counts; the thing that will
get you through the dark hours of the night

329

when the gray wolf of doubt, the prince
of fear, comes and sits on your chest and,
smiling, whispers to you, "Hello, friend.
I'm going to eat you, but you won't feel a
thing because I eat from the inside out."

Right about now, you're thinking, Is it
too late to get the guy with the foreign
policy speech?

Look, I'm exaggerating—but in spite
of how easy it is to say, "Commencement
means a beginning," I've learned in these
forty-seven years how bone-breakingly true
it is that today is just the beginning. The
rest of your life is going to be a continuing
education, whether you sign up for it or not.

There were two vitally important things
I learned in four years of college, and all
the rest has been built on those two things.
One was how to think more clearly, and
the other was how to use language better.
I remember with great satisfaction the
class in logic where I began to understand
that there were rules to thinking that,
if followed, could help you sort out
the illogicalities in someone's thinking,
especially your own. And even though I
was already trying to learn how to be a

writer, I remember the English class that truly invited me to dive headfirst into language. And that's it: logic and language. But that's all you need. The rest is experience.

No, there was one more thing I learned: that there were people who really cared if I learned. They invited me to exchange ignorance for curiosity. Now you'll notice I said curiosity and not knowledge or truth. That's because I think the opposite of ignorance is not just knowing something, it's being curious about it. A lot of the things we know for sure are really just rough drafts of reality. In a story set in Eden, Mark Twain has Eve say about Adam that he knows a multitude of things—which are mostly wrong. We haven't improved much since Adam.

I know this may all sound a little bleak, but what use would I be to you if I didn't tell you the real stuff? I'm happy and successful in every way that counts to me. So why don't I tell you how I got this way, and then you can be happy and successful, too. It'll be a well-spent afternoon, worth getting dressed up for.

Okay, this is important. Number one: Get verrry lucky.

Be lucky enough to find a person you love and work you love. Be lucky enough to be able to do that work as long as you want.

Number two: Have a backup in case number one doesn't work out. Be nimble.

You can't control the kind of luck you're going to get, but you can control what you do with it. I think making the most of what's come my way has been my greatest skill. I recommend it.

There are a few essential rules I've learned that I think have enabled me to make the most of what's come my way. For what they're worth, here they are . . . this won't take long, because I've only learned three things in my life.

Well, I've learned more than three things. I've learned some French and Italian, and I can say a few things in Chinese and Yiddish. I also know how to make rigatoni with artichokes—and these are all extremely useful skills. But they're not one of the three essentials. They won't save your life in an emergency—like suddenly growing old.

You can do these things whether you get lucky or not . . . in fact, getting lucky and not doing them is probably the best way to turn good luck into bad. These three essentials will help you make the most of what comes your way, whatever comes your way.

1. Make someone happy. Learn how to laugh and how to make someone else laugh. Take pleasure in who they are, as they are. In other words, love someone. Surrender to the person you love. I don't mean give in. I mean surrender. Put down the arms of war and open the other kind. You don't need to debate and compromise with someone you love. Just make them happy.

2. Find out how you can be helpful. It didn't occur to me at first that being helpful was better than being the center of attention. That's not an idea that would tend to occur to an actor. But it turns out that if you can really find a way to be helpful, more satisfaction and praise than

you know what to do with will come your way. Being helpful assumes that the people you help actually want your help. And that you know enough to actually be of help and not make life worse for them than it already is. This means getting as smart as you can. But getting smart is a tricky business. The smartest people I've ever met are the ones who knew exactly what they were ignorant of. If you don't know much about something, assuming that what little you know is all there is to know is not the way to find out more. And try not to assume you can just take a stab at complex things. Complex things bite. So be wary of simple answers to complex questions.

3. If you keep score, keep score your way. Don't let the world tell you success is a big house if you think success is a happy home. If you meet a bully who says, "I'm stronger and richer than you, and you're nothing

if you're not richer or stronger than I am," and if he's richer and stronger than you'll ever be, wouldn't it be stupid to get into a pissing contest with this guy?

But maybe I'm putting it into too many words. Let's say I was about to be shot in some penny ante dictatorship and the firing squad says, "You have ten seconds to tell us everything you know. And if you can't do it in one sentence, the president told us to shoot you." Here's what I'd say: "Boys, think for yourselves."

I think that sums up everything but the love part.

Thinking it through is what I'm asking of you. No matter what the ideology is, get the facts. Don't just rely on your beliefs. Everything is more complex than it first seems, and being passionate doesn't make you right.

Now, about being the leaders of tomorrow: Given the way the world works, how could you, sitting here today, take seriously the words of some character up here saying, "You are the leaders of tomorrow—you are our future"?

Let's be serious. When you leave here, if you're lucky enough to find a job, you'll spend the next ten years learning the ropes and finding out exactly what compromises to make to get ahead. You'll learn how to make and sell cars that are a little less safe than you personally would like to drive— you'll make movies that are a little more stupid and predictable than you would like to see—you'll fly people in planes with just a little more time between safety inspections than you yourself feel comfortable with. You'll do this because the system you're trying to fit into has been in place for longer than your ideals have. It's the one your parents had to adjust to in order to survive—and their parents, too.

The single greatest American invention was not Henry Ford's car—it was Henry Ford's assembly line. In our time, it's reached the peak of perfection. Everyone on the line has a specialized role to play. Crank your nut, slam in your bolt, and go home. No one is responsible for the whole thing, just his or her little part of it. It only has to be good enough to sell—and its value, its worth, is reckoned by the price it gets. Your ambition will be directed at getting a better place on the assembly line and someday maybe even running the line—but as in that great Lily Tomlin aphorism, "The trouble with the rat race is even if you win, you're still a rat."

So what chance do you have to be "our future"?

This chance: You can decide to think for yourself. You can say to yourself, I will make a silk purse out of every sow's ear that comes down the assembly line.

You may be expected to tell people only what they need to know to make the sale. But if you learn to find out what they actually need and help them get it, I bet you'll feel better and even do better. It takes more energy—much more energy—but it's also more fun. Edmund Burke said: "The only thing necessary for the triumph of evil is for good men to do nothing." And I say the only thing necessary for the triumph of the assembly line is for creative people with the energy of youth to do nothing but learn the ropes.

So that's it. I've told you everything I know.

Think clearly and think for yourself; learn to use language to express those thoughts. Love somebody with all your heart . . . and with everyone, whether you love them or not, find out how you can be helpful.

But, really, it's even simpler than that. After all this time, and all these talks in public and in private, I think I get it now. If I were taking my friend Arnold's suggestion and spoke from my deathbed, I think I know what I'd say: I see now that I had my meaning all along. I just had to notice it.

The meaning of life is life.

Not **noticing** life is what's meaningless, right down to the last second. When I played Richard Feynman on the stage, Feynman, who was dying of cancer, told his doctor he didn't want an anesthetic at the end, because "if I'm going to die, I want to be there when I do." Even in this last moment, there will be something to notice. After all the talk, **that's** the final word.

Notice.

So, go. Accomplish as much as you can. But while you're busy doing great things—don't forget to tend to Bosco's belly.

ABOUT THE AUTHOR

ALAN ALDA played Hawkeye Pierce for eleven years in the television series M*A*S*H and has acted in, written, and directed many feature films. He has starred often on Broadway, and his avid interest in science has led to his hosting PBS's **Scientific American Frontiers** for eleven years. He was nominated for an Academy Award in 2005 and has been nominated for thirty-two (and has won six) Emmy Awards. He is married to the children's book author and photographer Arlene Alda. They have three grown children and seven grandchildren.

LIKE WHAT YOU'VE SEEN?

If you enjoyed this large print edition of
**THINGS I OVERHEARD WHILE
TALKING TO MYSELF**, here is another book
by Alan Alda available in large print.

NEVER HAVE YOUR DOG STUFFED
(hardcover)
978-0-7393-2552-0 • 0-7393-2552-3
$26.95/$37.95C

Large print books are available wherever books
are sold and at many local libraries.

All prices are subject to change. Check with your
local retailer for current pricing and availability.
For more information on these and other large print titles,
visit www.randomhouse.com/largeprint.